KLONDIKE IN COLOR

GRAHAM WILSON

Klondike In Color

Copyright © 2014 by Graham Wilson.

ISBN: 978-1-927691-08-3

Printed in Canada.

Photograph Coloring: Hrach Drambyan.

Text Editing: Amelia Gilliland.

Front Cover Photograph: Portrait of "Klondike Kate" Rockwell, an entertainer who was popular in Dawson City.

No part of this book may be reproduced, stored in a retrieval system, or transmitted in any form, by any means, without the prior permission of the publisher, except by a reviewer, who may quote brief passages in a review.

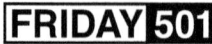

Box 31599, Whitehorse, Yukon, Canada, Y1A 6L2
www.friday501.com, info@friday501.com

When the small steamship *Excelsior* docked in San Francisco in July 1897, the world was watching. Aboard this vessel were millionaires who had been penniless men only months before. A few days later the steamship *Portland* landed at Seattle with sixty-eight miners and almost a ton of gold. The news of the find grabbed newspaper headlines and was on everyone's lips. Overnight, the word "Klondike" took on mythic proportions.

Within days thousands flocked to west coast towns from San Francisco to Vancouver trying to book passage north. The fact that the Klondike was more than fifteen hundred miles away and over a precipitous mountain pass would not deter many. Gold fever had grasped the nation, and everyone wanted the chance to try their luck in the new frontier. As the wealthy veterans of the Klondike bought rounds of drinks in the bars of San Francisco and Seattle, thousands planned their passage to the gold fields. The rush was on. A gold rush like no other.

The Stampeders traveled up the coast to Alaska in overcrowded and often decrepit ships. They spent the winter ferrying supplies over the frigid and dangerous Chilkoot Pass and built rickety boats and navigated the lakes and rapids of the Yukon River system. Once in Dawson City a fortunate few worked claims and struck it rich. Most Stampeders left the Yukon broke but had a lifetime of stories to tell.

The process to color these photographs required much careful attention. The first step was to remove imperfections such as dust and scratches and add contrast and tonal depth. Next, realistic colors were painstakingly added using modern digital techniques. The goal was to maintain the original photograph's integrity and establish an aesthetic that is thematically correct. The result is a collection that looks and feels strangely contemporary. The Stampeders endured unimaginable hardships and took great risks. Some were killed by the trail and others traumatized by the rigors of the ordeal. It is with the greatest respect that these images were prepared.

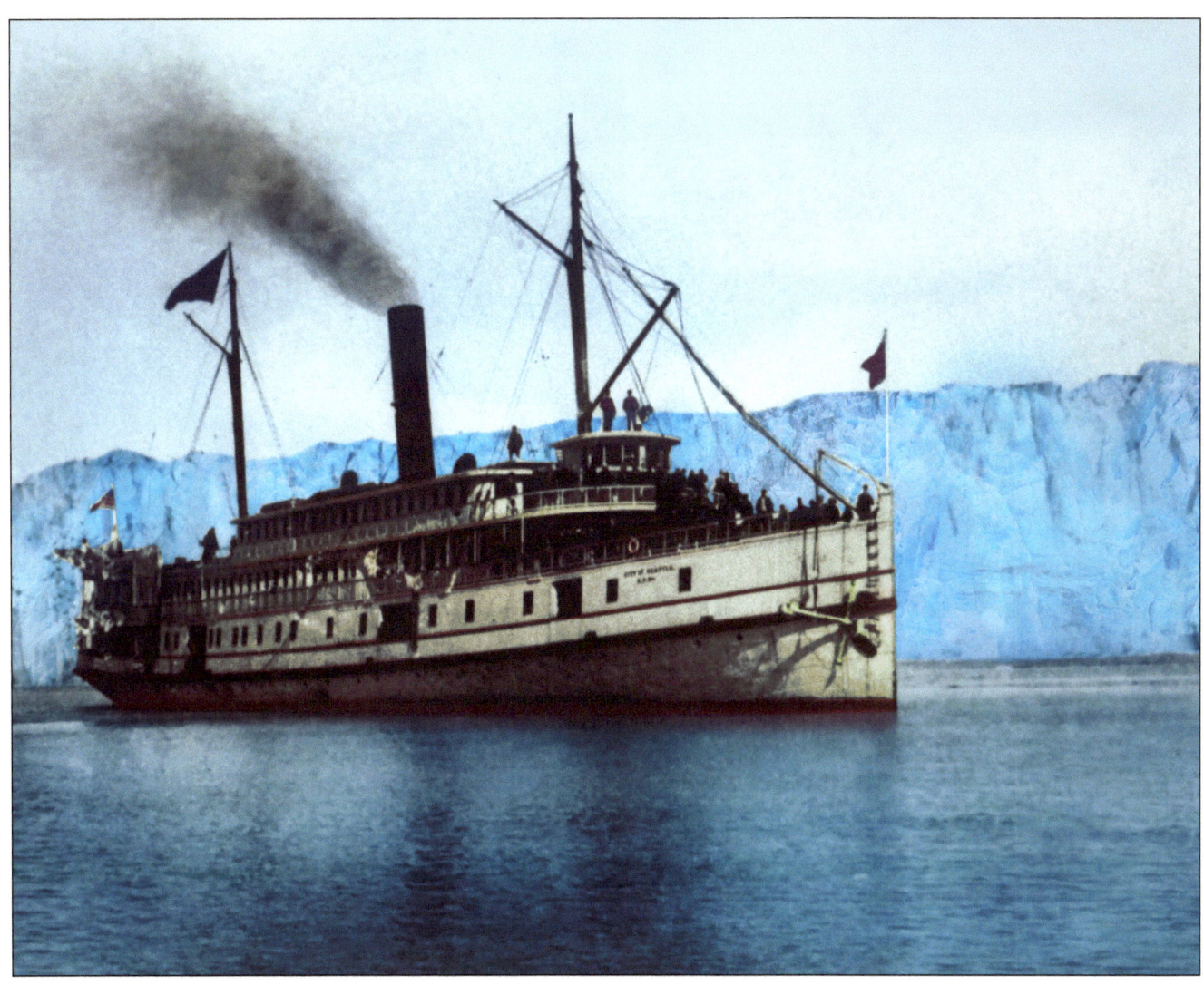

Above: Steamships carried tens of thousands of Stampeders to Alaska. The City of Seattle, in Glacier Bay, Alaska, with Muir Glacier in the background. Even the most rickety and worn-out steamships were pressed into service to bring eager passengers. Many of these ships were poorly provisioned and overcrowded for the race north.

Pages 6 and 7: Stampeders amid mountains of supplies landed near the mouth of the Taiya River near Dyea, Alaska. Ships landing at Dyea anchored offshore and scows carried the miners supplies to the beach. Once on the beach miner's had to race the tide to get their supplies a mile up the beach and away from the destructive forces of the ocean.

Fearing starvation in the gold fields the Canadian government only allowed entry to Stampeders with a ton of provisions. It was believed that a ton of food could feed a man for a year in the Klondike.

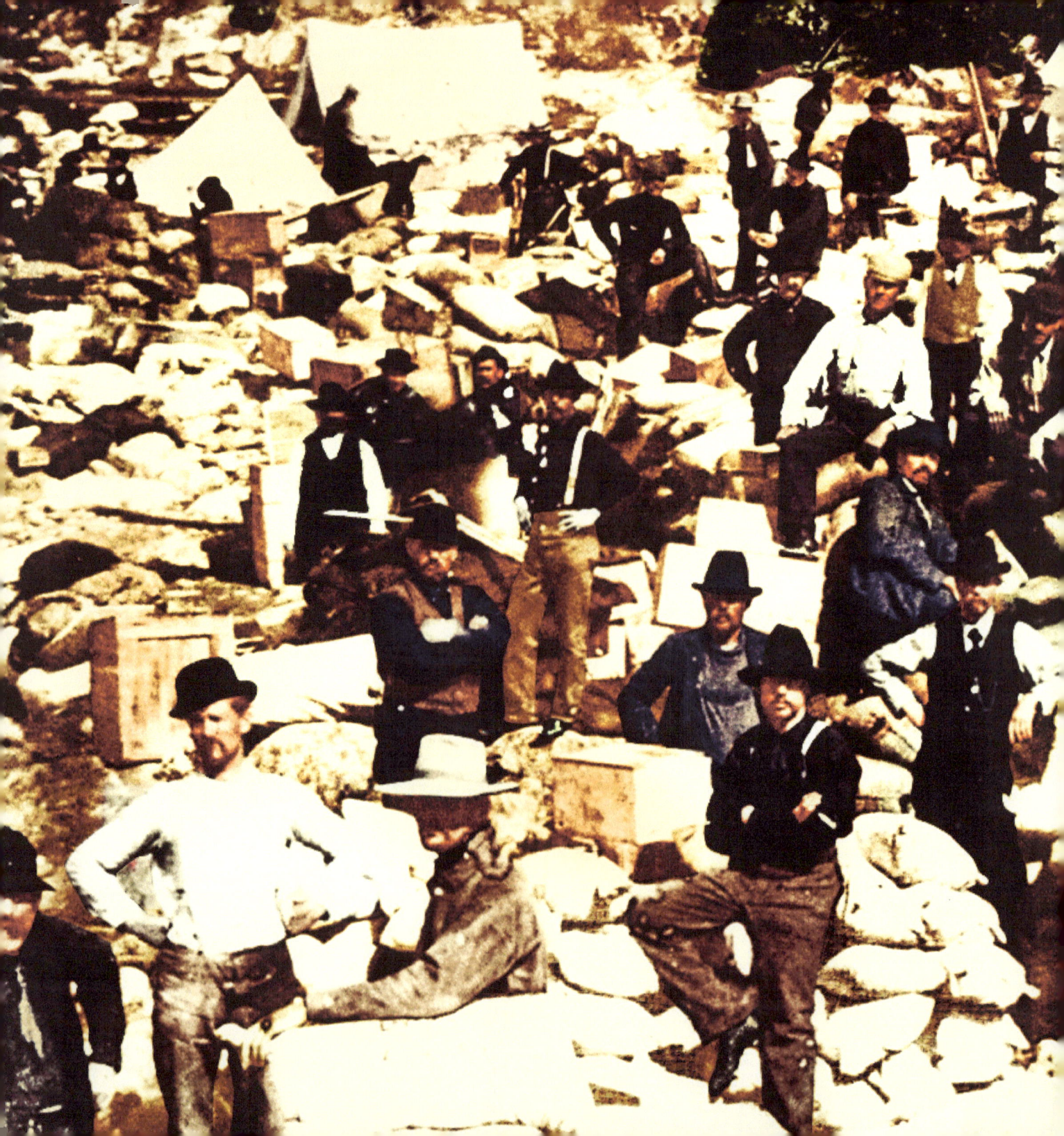

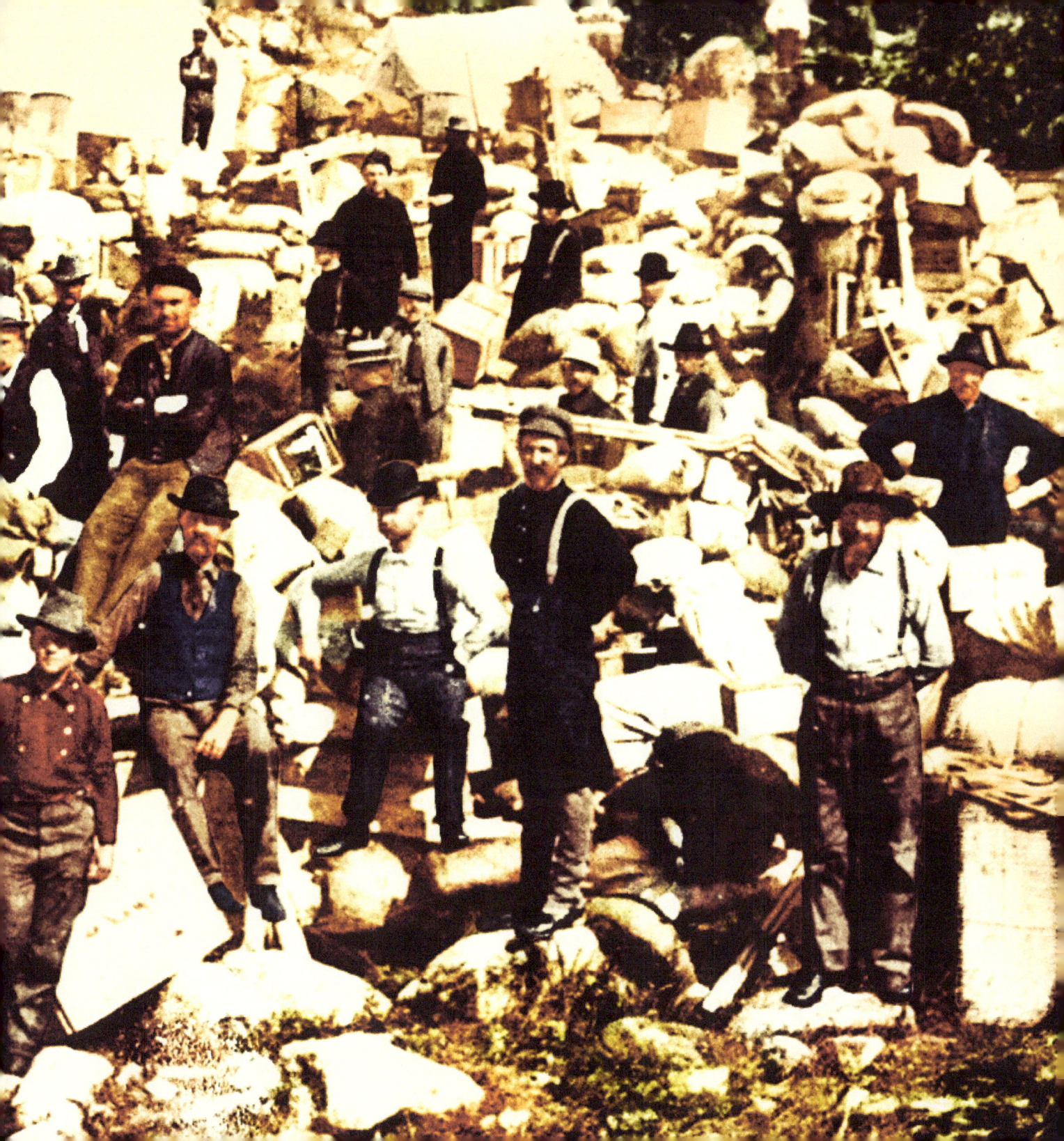

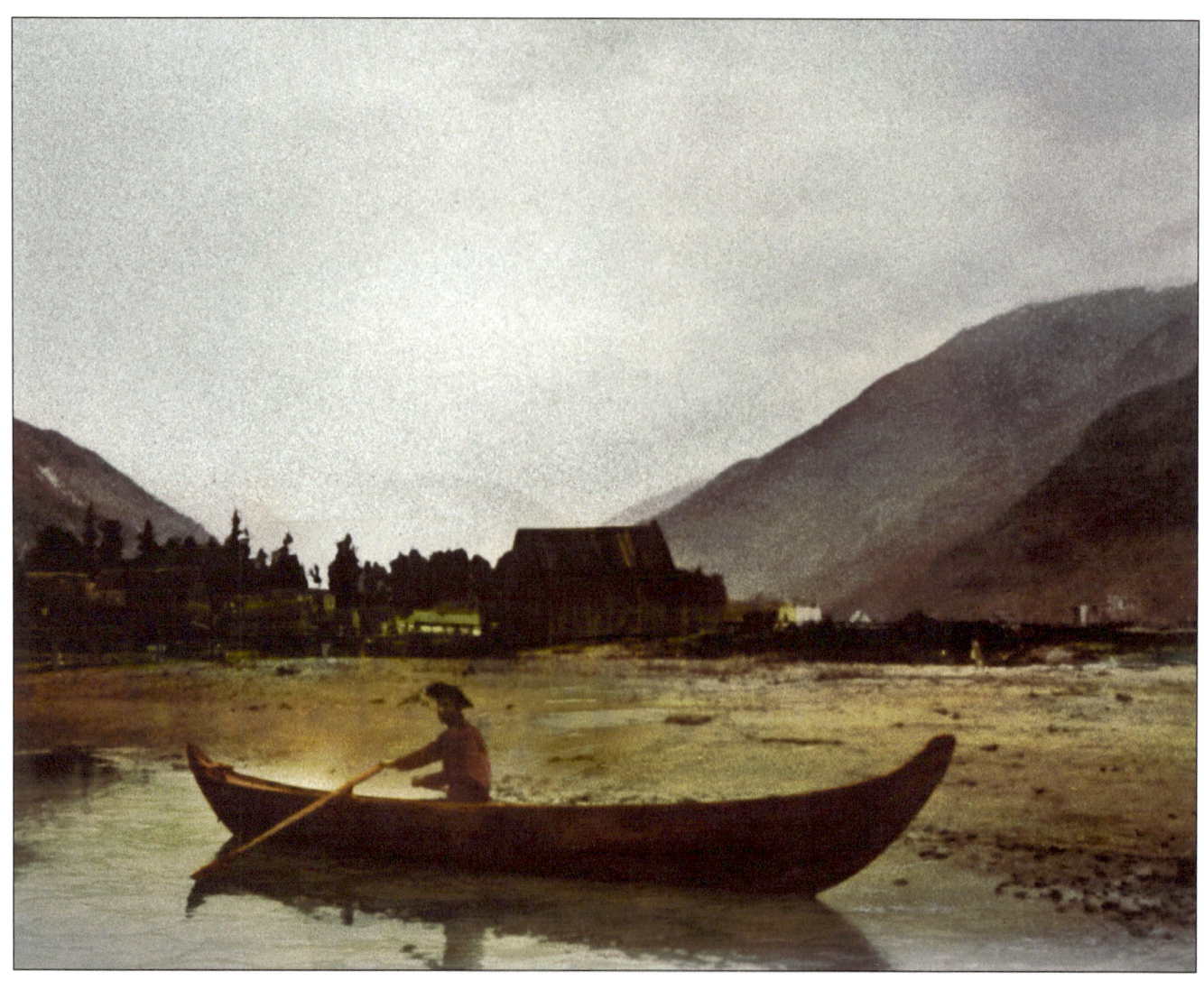

Above: Partial view of Dyea with a Chilkat Indian canoe on the Taiya River in the foreground. At its peak there were 150 businesses in Dyea including 48 hotels. Not a single building in this picture is standing today. The Chilkoot Pass has been used as a corridor to the interior by Indians for millennia.

Opposite: "Chilkoot Jack," a Chilkat Indian Chief, guided many over the Chilkoot Pass to the Yukon. He is pictured here wearing ceremonial dress. Despite gold being discovered by an aboriginal man, Skookum Jim, relatively few aboriginal people benefitted materially from the Gold Rush. The diseases, environmental damage and social impacts of the Gold Rush led to much suffering in the Indian community.

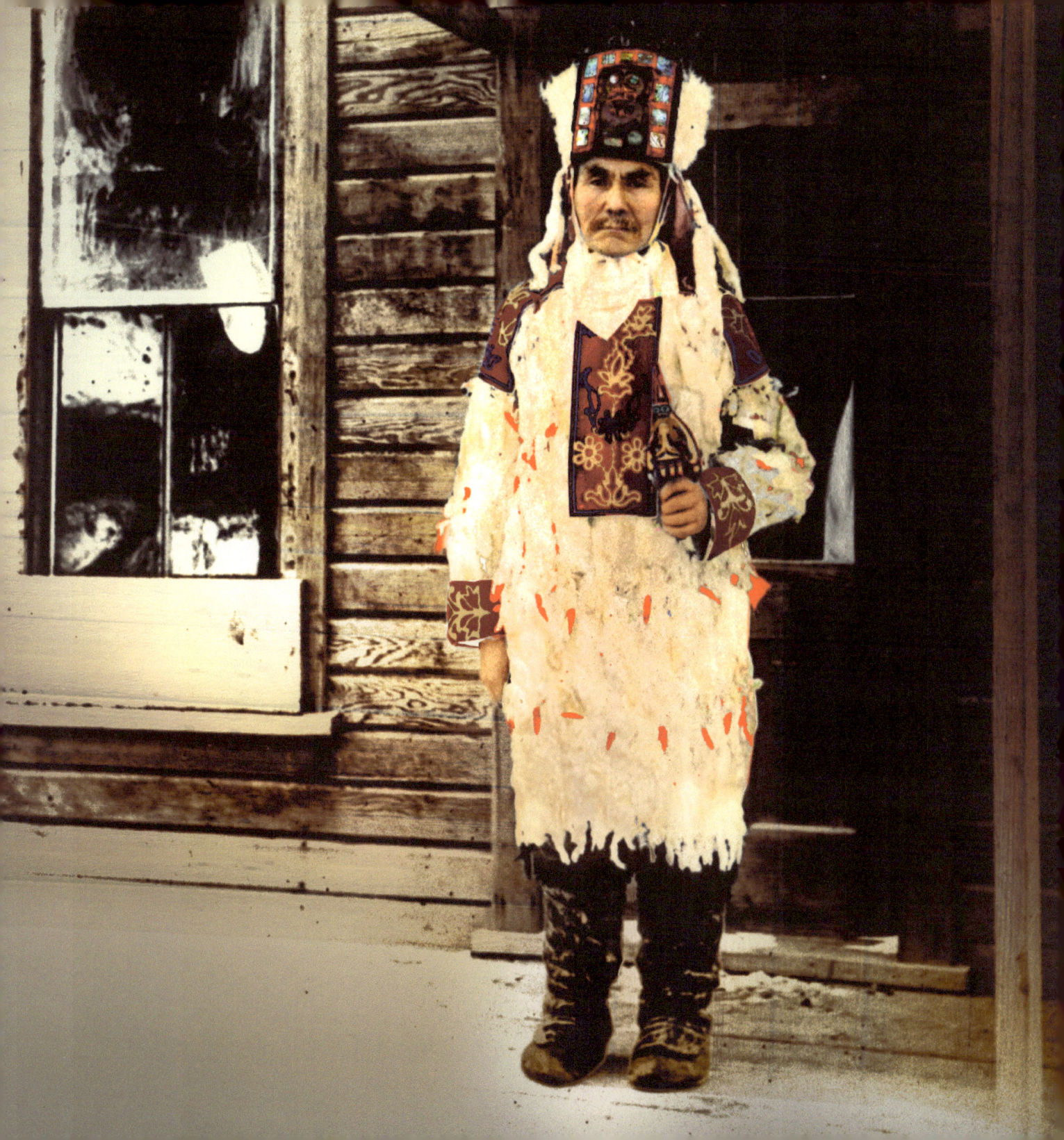

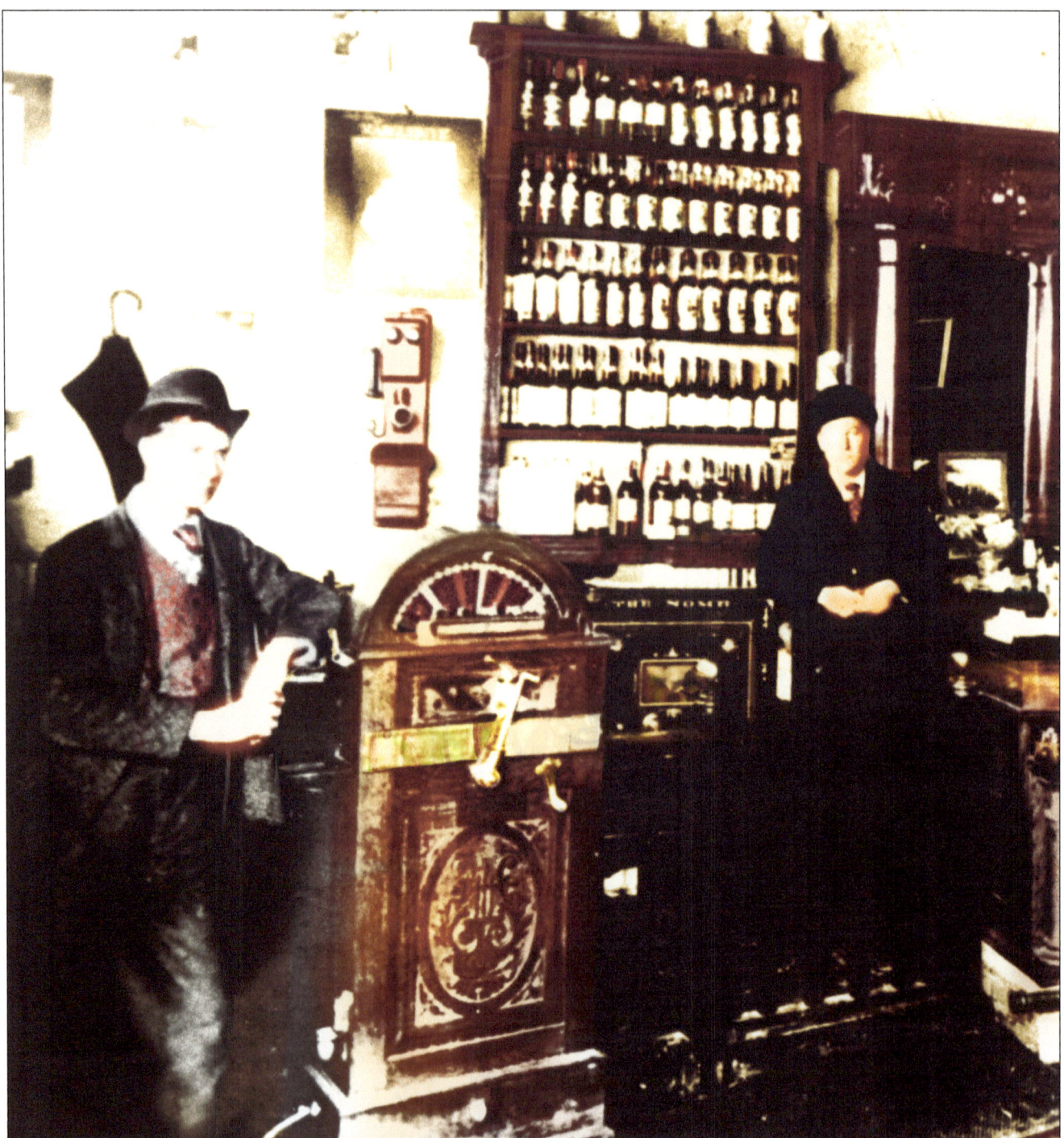

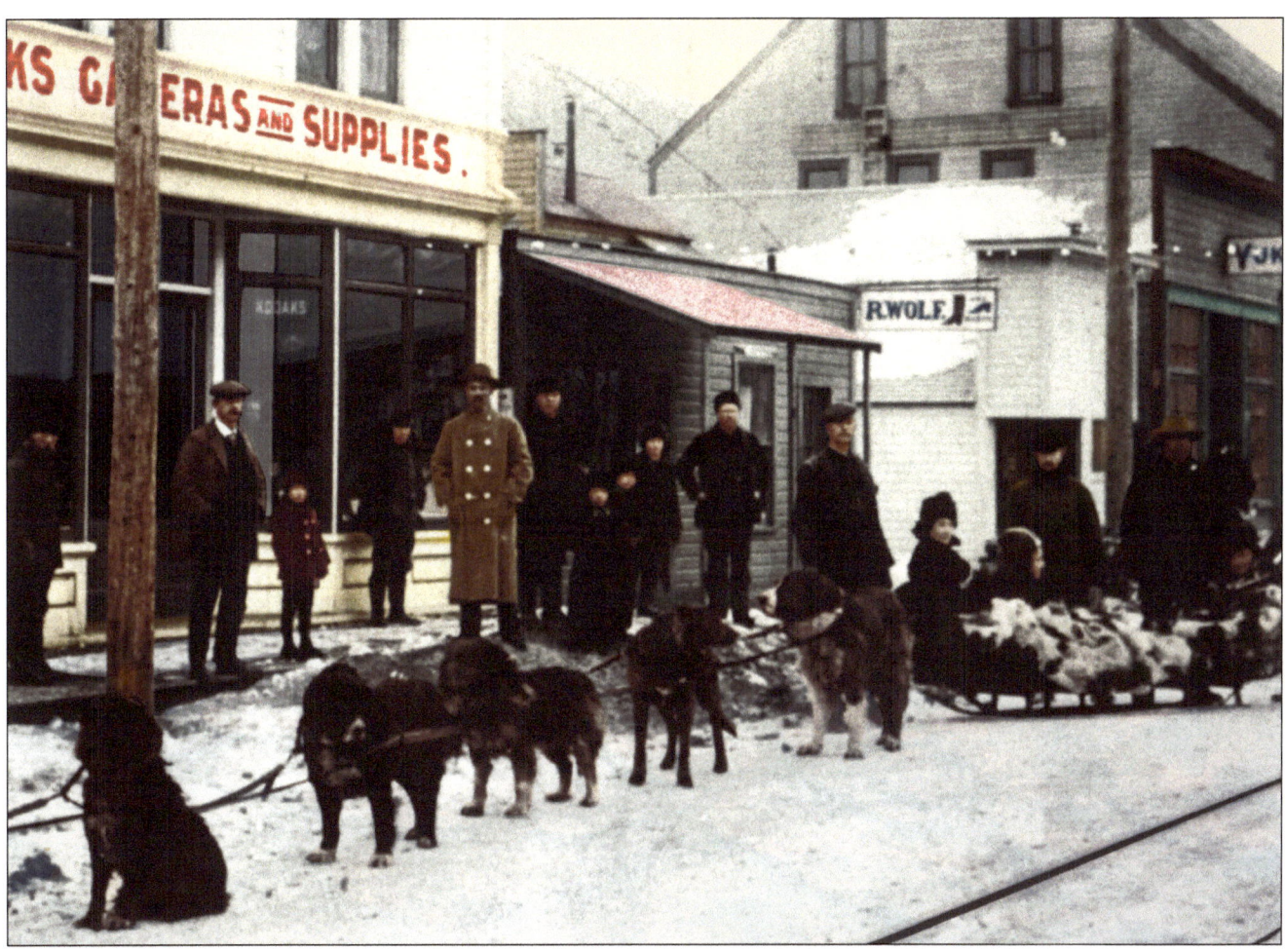

Above: Dog team in front of Case & Draper Photography store in Skagway. Sled dogs were a reliable mode of transportation in the north.

In the first couple of years of the gold rush, Skagway was the type of frontier town we see in western movies. It had makeshift buildings with false fronts, gambling halls, saloons, dance halls and bandits.

Opposite: Nome Saloon in Skagway. The towns of Skagway and Dyea sprang almost instantly from the tidal flats of the Lynn Canal. Skagway was the start of the White Pass Trail and Dyea was the start of the Chilkoot Trail. They were the most popular routes to the Klondike gold fields. For many Stampeders this was their first glimpse of the ordeal ahead of them. Some booked passage home, choosing to cut their losses.

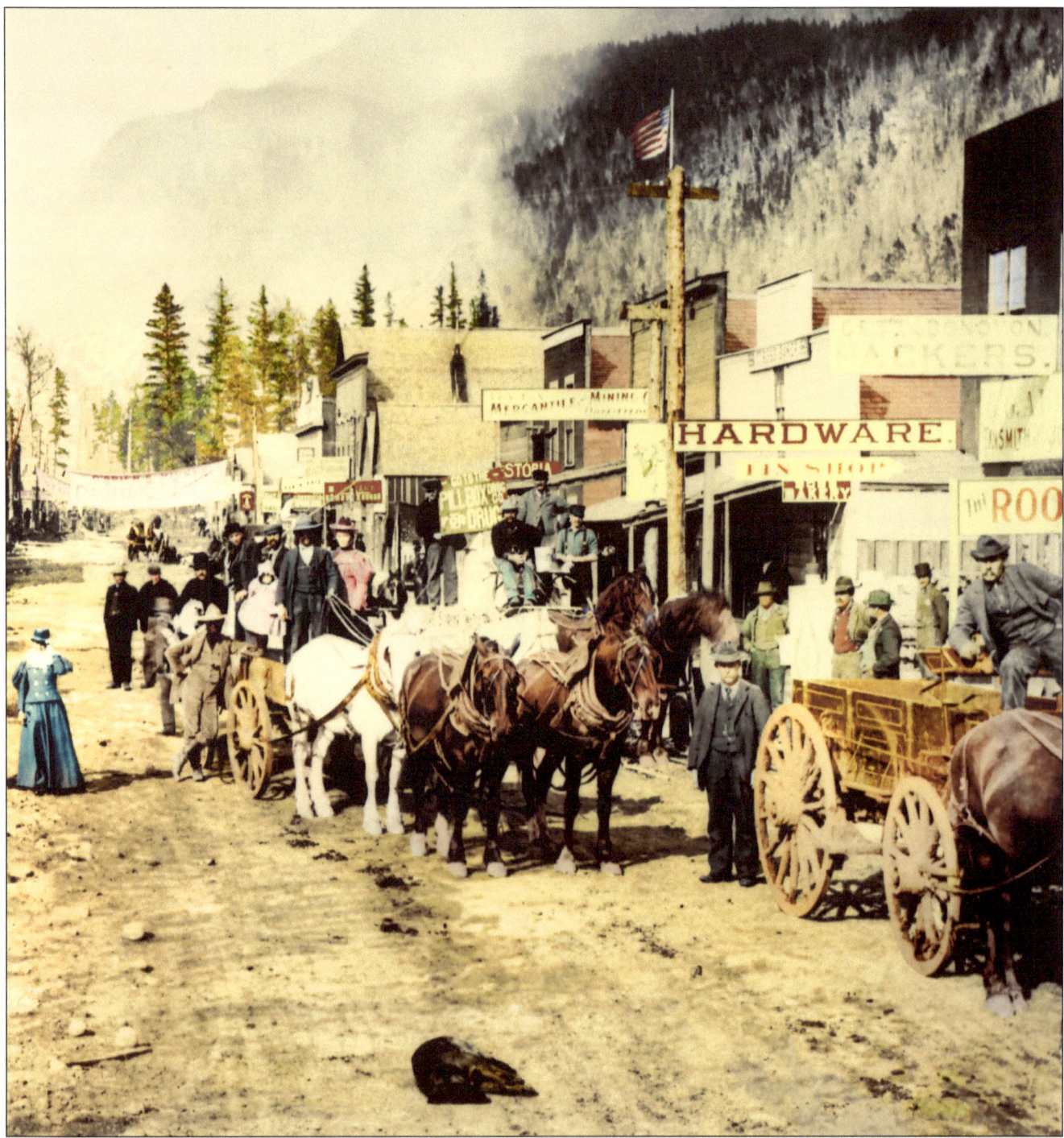

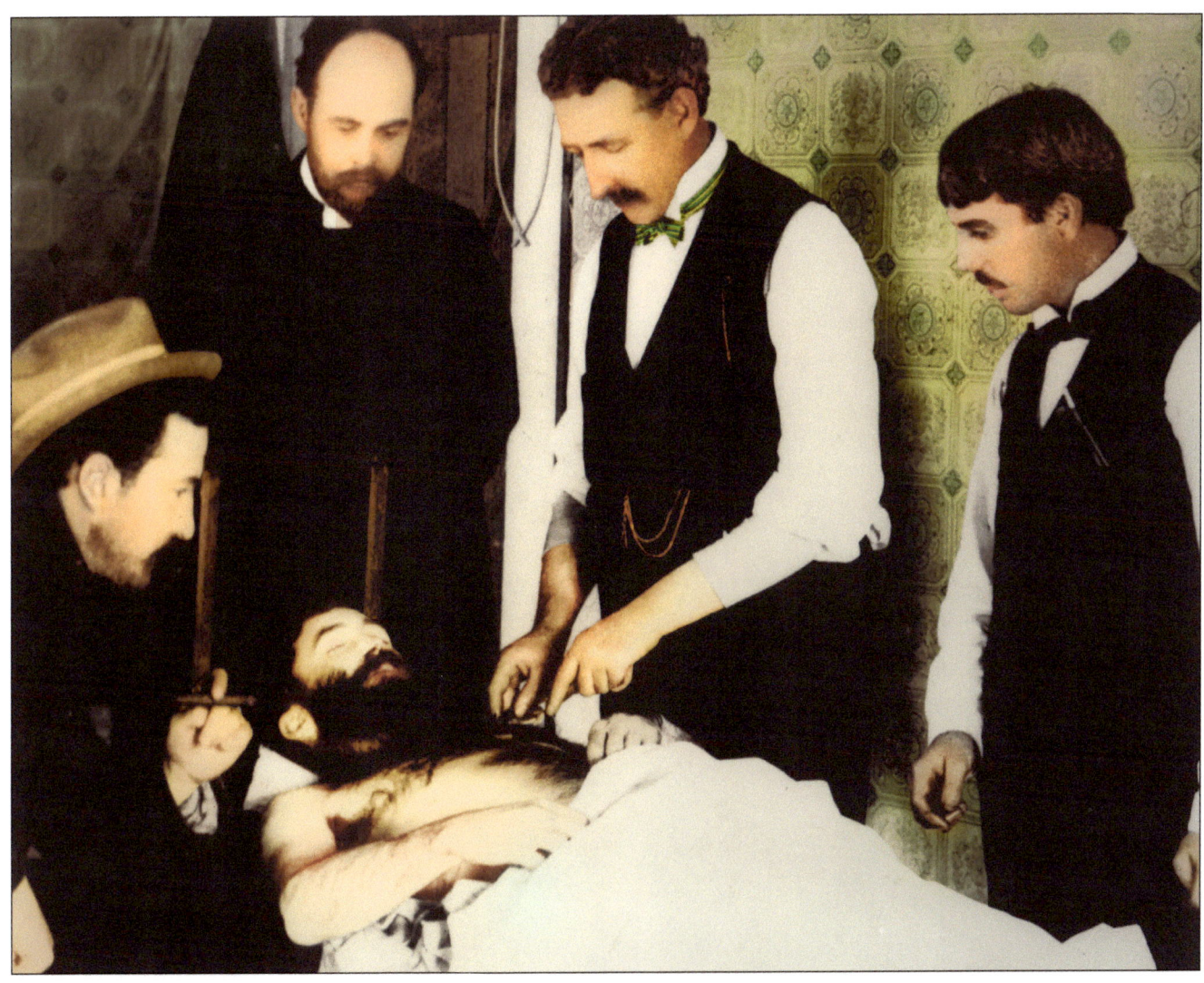

Above: Notorious gangster Jefferson "Soapy" Smith as seen at his autopsy. Soapy's gang of bandits were experienced con men and thieves, many of whom were veterans from other gold rushes. Skagway was an outlaw's haven and Soapy's gang conned, cheated and stole from Stampeders at will. On July 8, 1898, a vigilante group formed to put an end to Soapy's empire. A gunfight followed, leaving Soapy dead, and a short time later his assailant Frank Reid also died. At Soapy's funeral the minister recited from Proverbs: "The way of transgressors is hard."

Opposite: Crowd on Main Street, Skagway, waiting for their mail. By the spring of 1898 Skagway had a population of 10,000 and was the largest city in Alaska. More than a thousand Stampeders passed through town each week on their way to the Yukon.

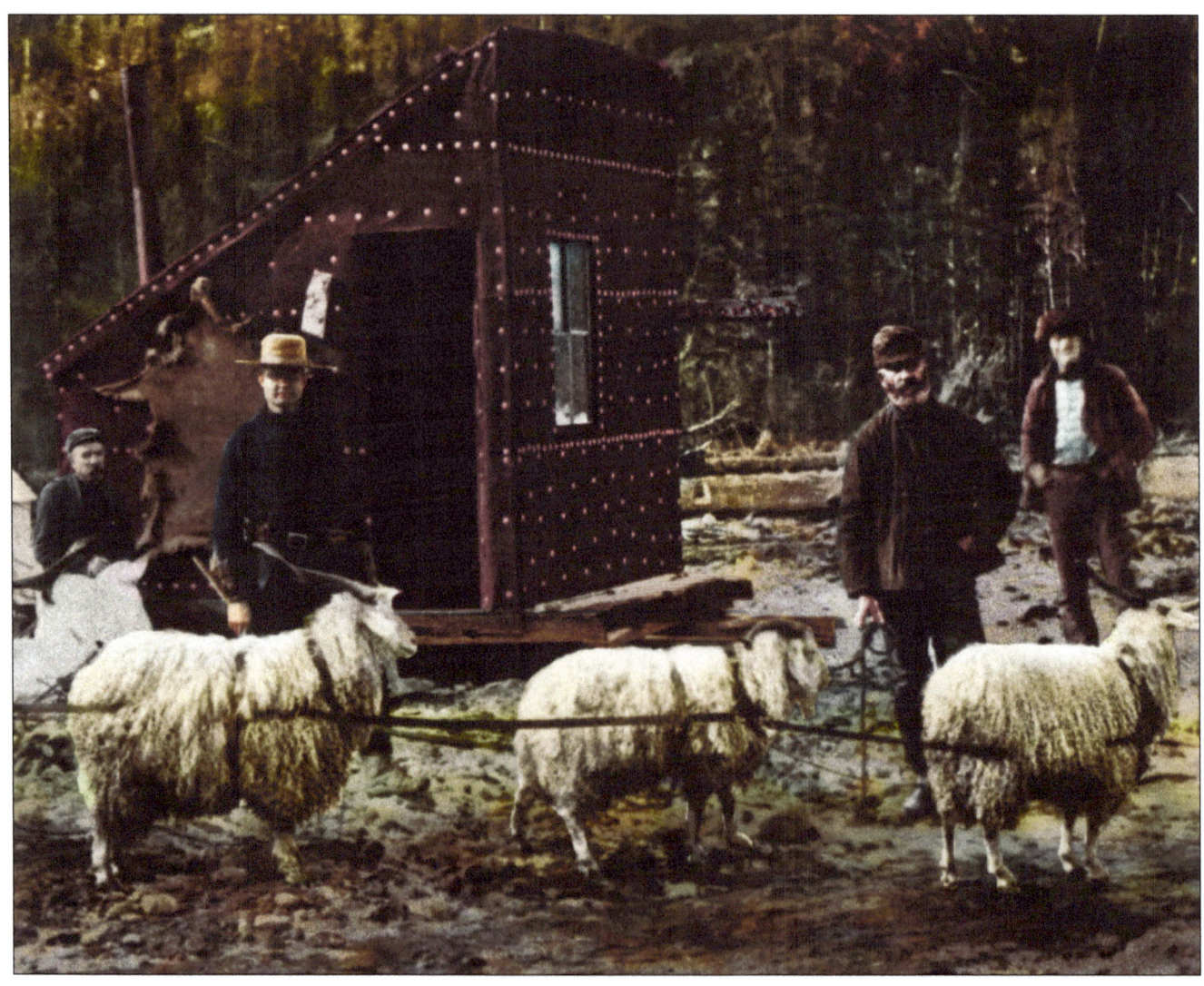

Above: A sled of supplies en route to the Klondike being pulled by a team of goats.

Opposite: An ox loaded with supplies. Almost anything that would pull a sled or carry a pack was recruited. The White Pass Trail was steep and had numerous sink-holes where horses and other pack animals easily broke ankles or were impaled by stumps. Gold fever drove Stampeders to abuse their half-starved horses in the most horrible manner. For this reason the White Pass became known as the trail of "Dead Horses." It is estimated that as many as 3,000 horses may have died during the first year of the gold rush.

By most accounts the Chilkoot was the preferred trail to the interior. The Chilkoot gained its elevation more gradually and traversed a broader valley. However, the Chilkoot was still a challenging obstacle that sent many Stampeders home before even reaching the alpine.

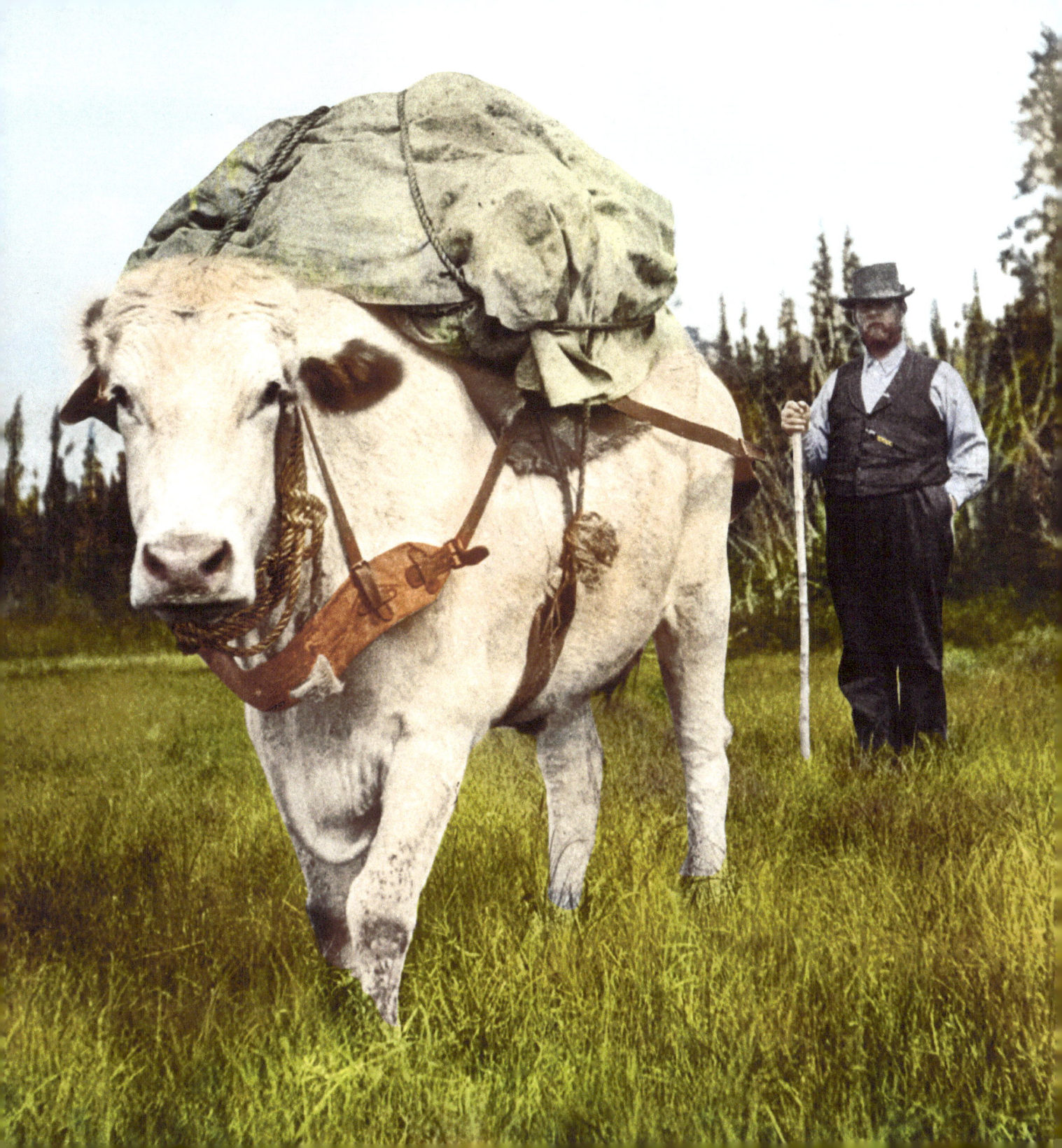

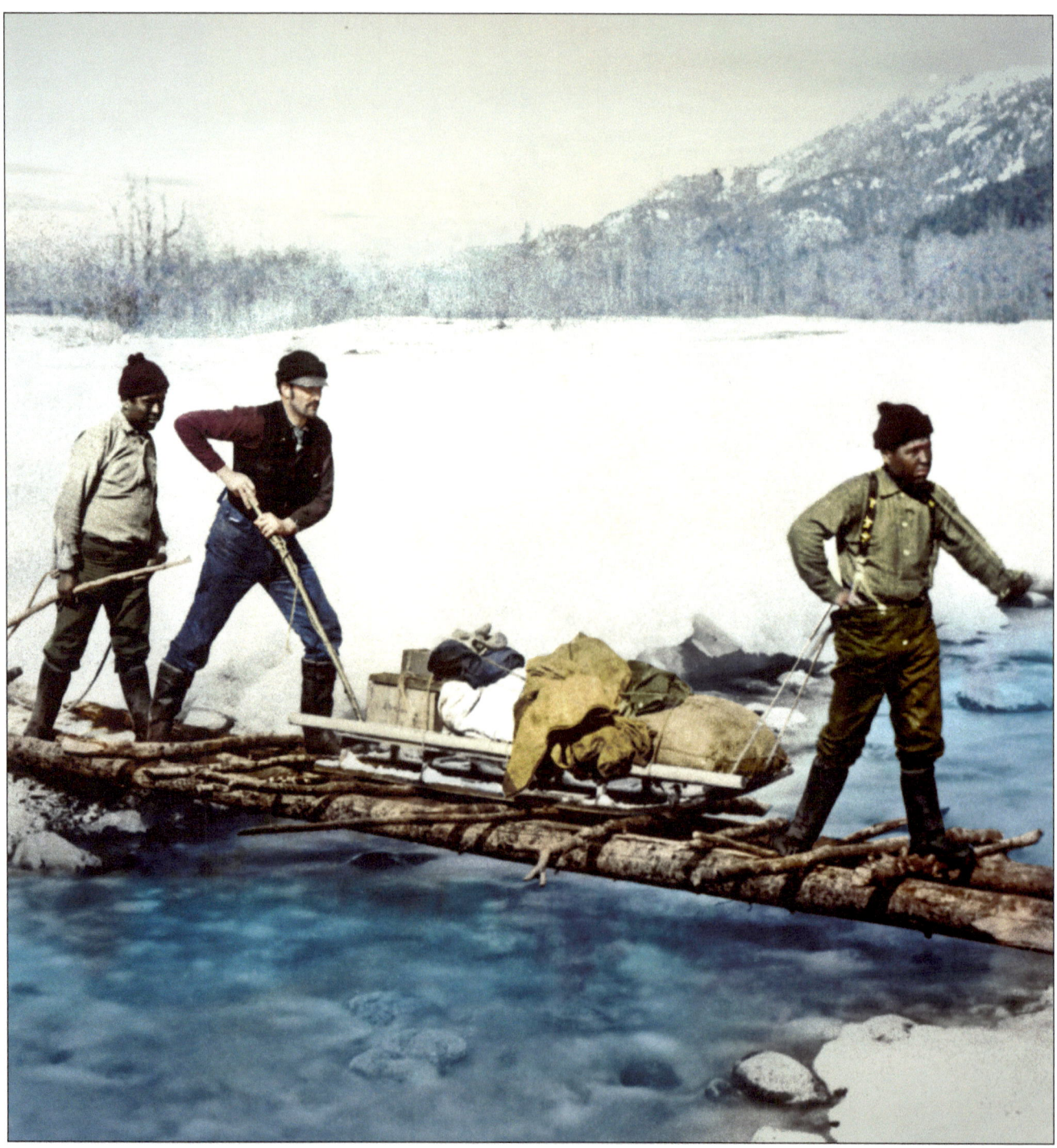

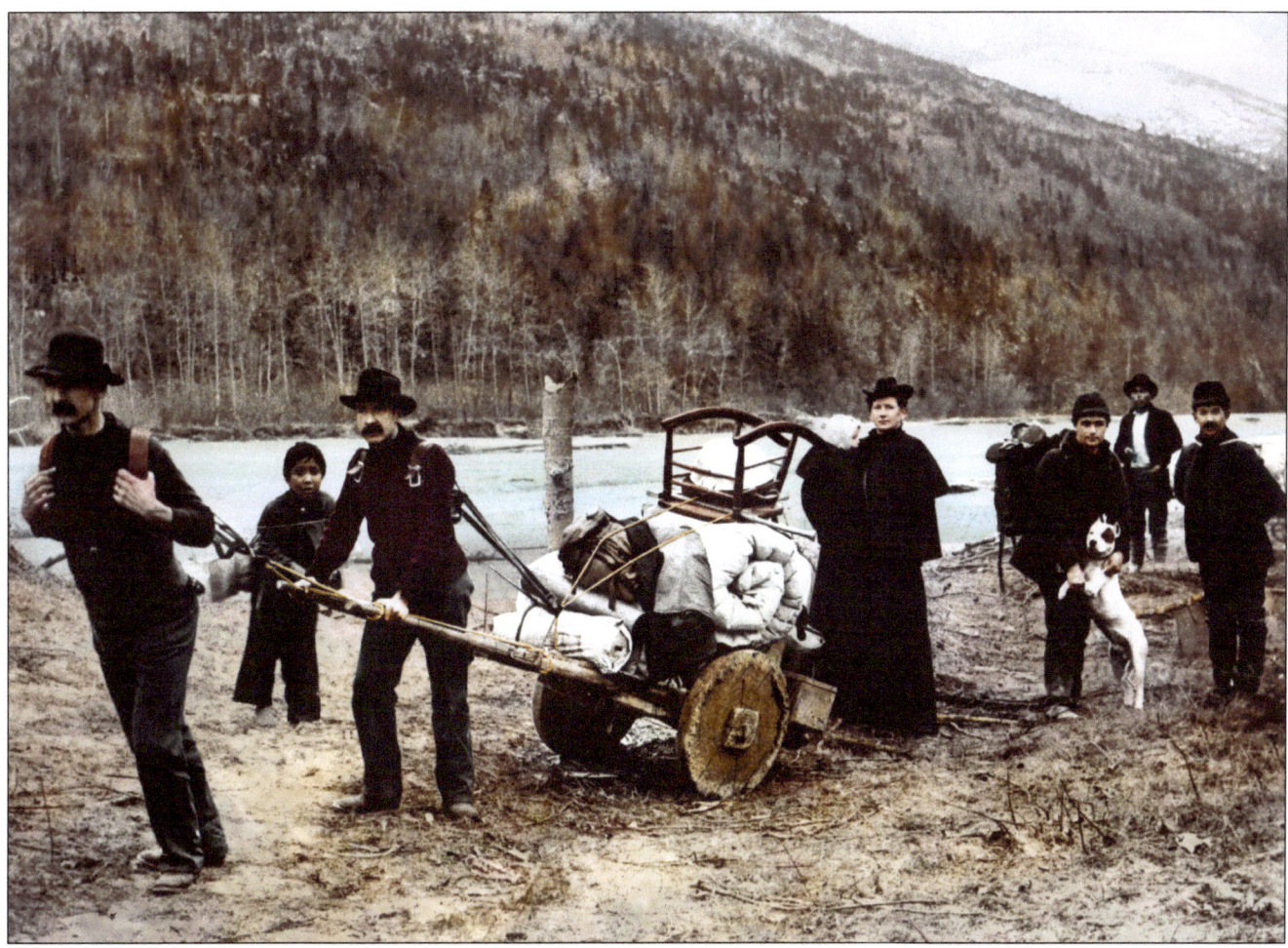

Above: Family carrying heavy packs and pulling a handcart at the start of the Chilkoot Trail. The trail was soon littered with anything other than the most essential supplies. The rocking chair on top of the cart likely did not cross the pass.

Opposite: Two Indian packers with Alaskan photographer Lloyd Winter crossing a log bridge. Many Indian men and women were hired as porters on the Chilkoot Trail.

The rugged experience of climbing these passes haunted many Stampeders for the rest of their lives. The frequently harsh alpine conditions only exacerbated the challenges. To haul the required year of provisions meant Stampeders had to relay heavy packs along the trail. This required each person to make an average of twenty to thirty trips along this trail. The wealthy could hire Indian packers or later in the rush use a tramway to carry supplies. However, most stampeders simply put their heads down and grunted their boxes, bags and satchels over the pass. Many took several months to complete the Chilkoot. By 1900 the White Pass and Yukon Route railway was completed through the White Pass Valley to Whitehorse. Subsequently these trails were abandoned.

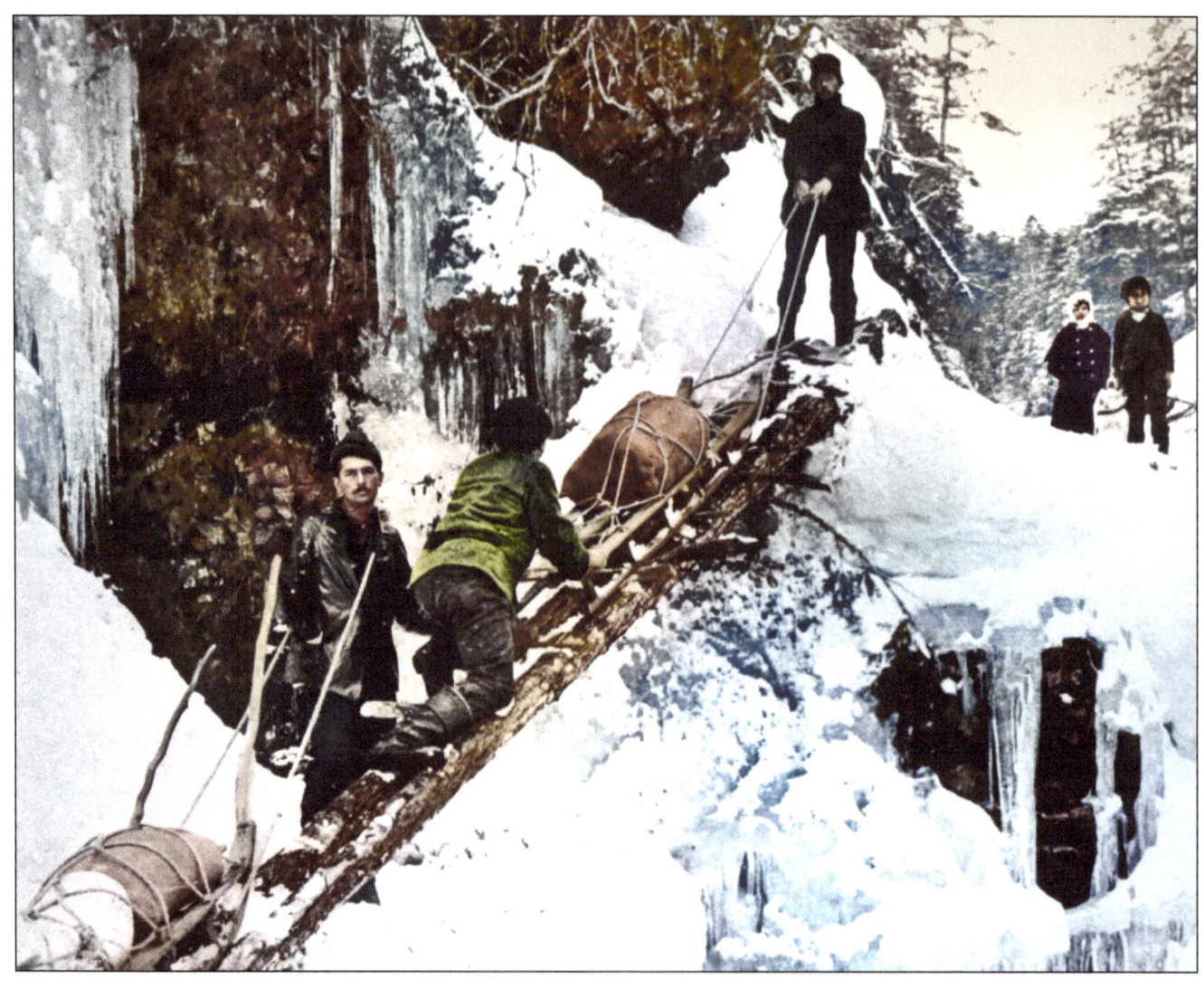

Above: Stampeders hauling sleds up "Jacob's Ladder," in a canyon near Sheep Camp on the Chilkoot Trail. The worst season to travel the trail was during the winter as sub-zero temperatures, high winds and blizzards stopped many in their tracks. The winter of 1897 - 98 was particularly harsh with extraordinarily high amounts of snow accumulating on the summit of the Chilkoot. Overnight, entire communities of tents and supplies were buried under mountains of snow. The Chilkoot was a dangerous place where horrible suffering was a daily reality.

Opposite: Men and women pulling sleds through the Dyea Canyon.

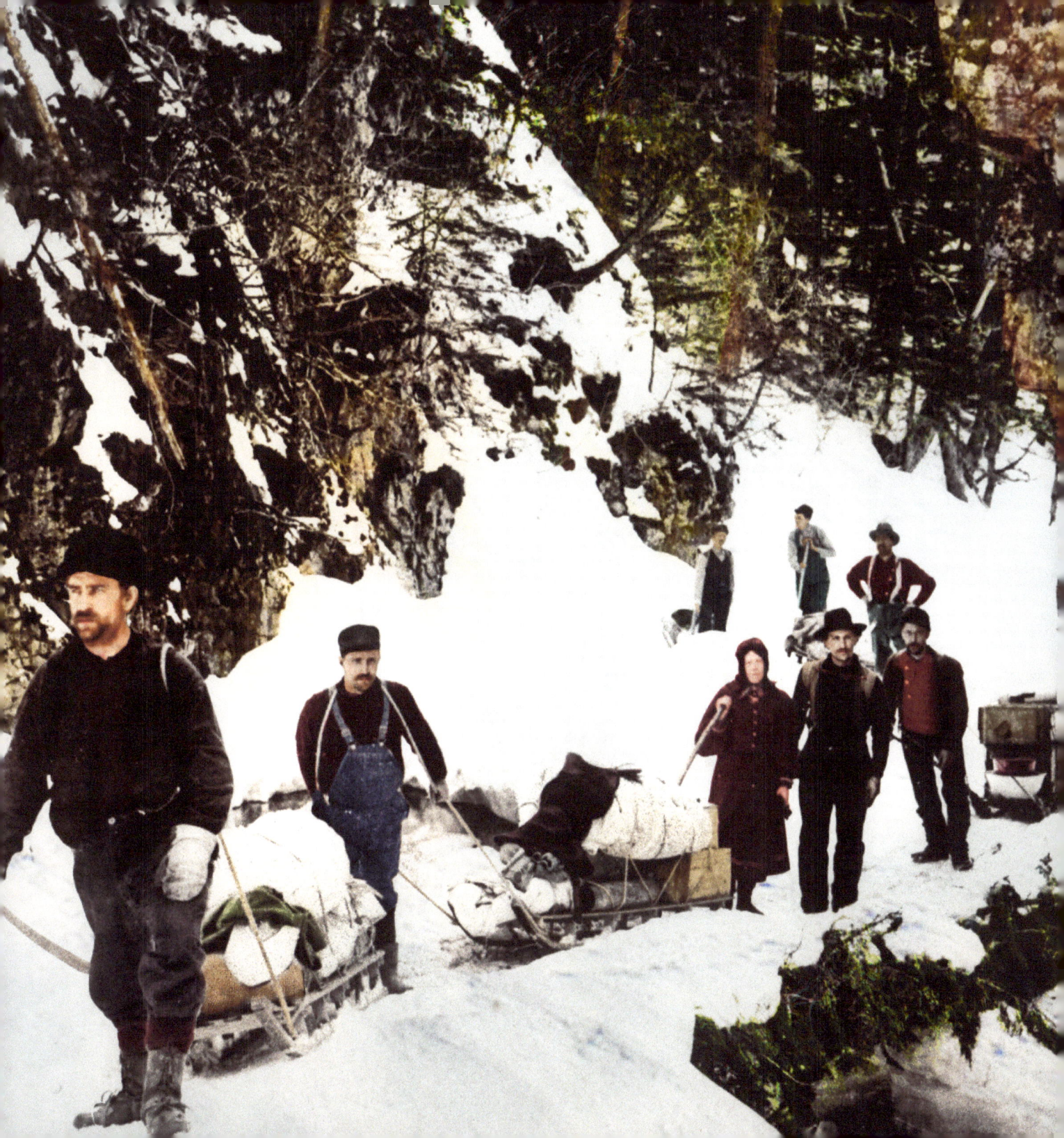

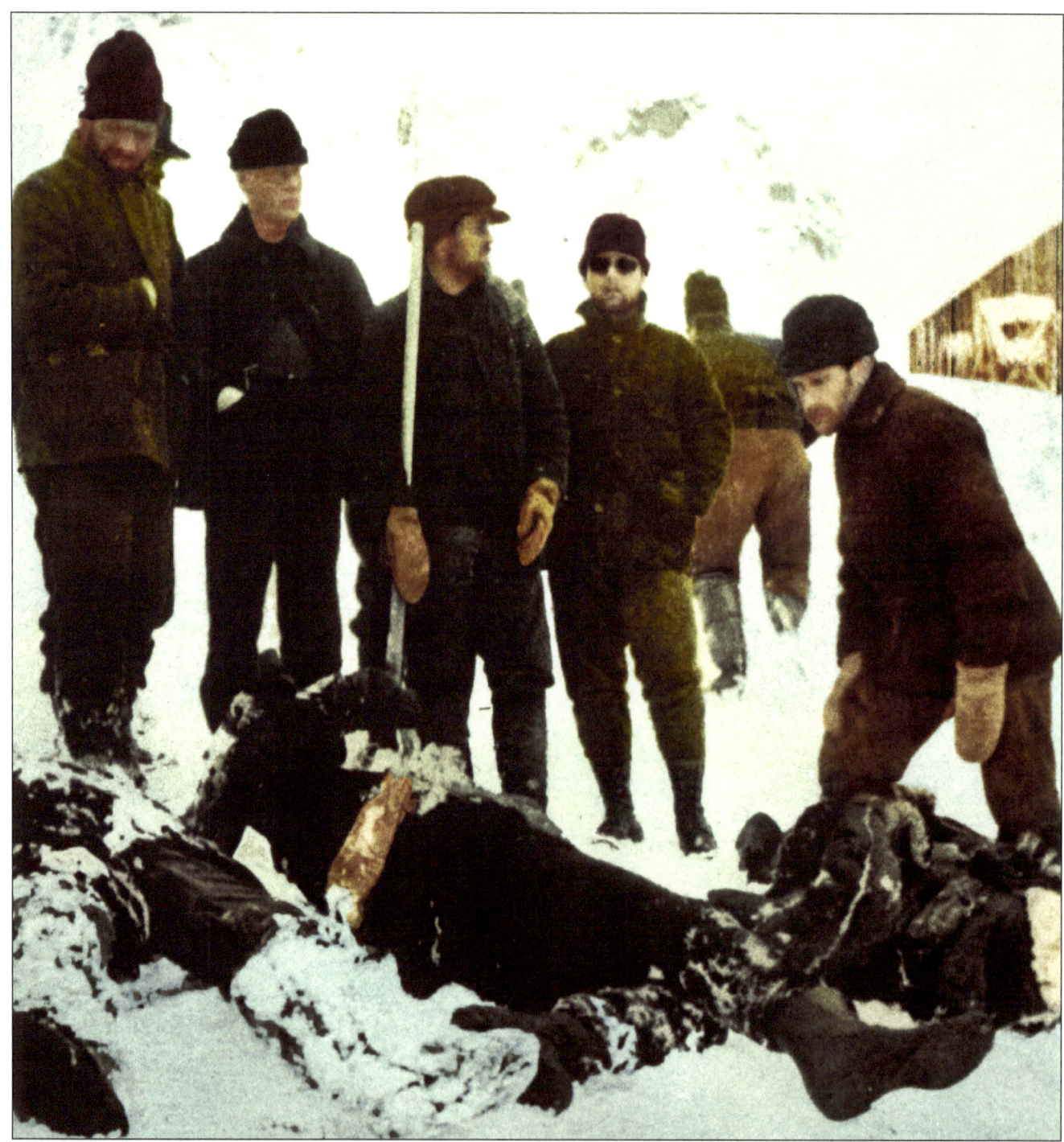

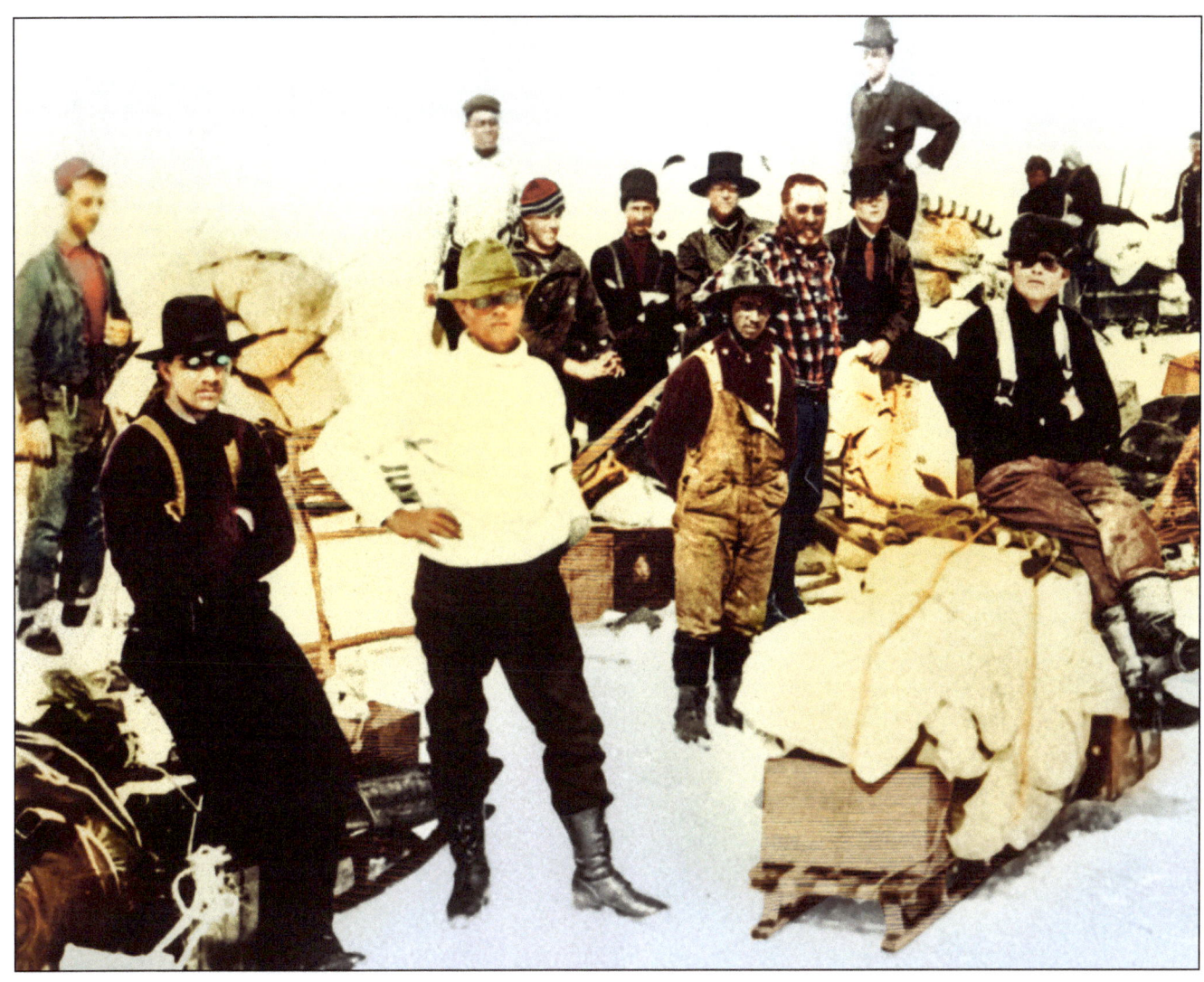

Above: A group of Stampeders with loaded sleds and caches of supplies.

Opposite: On April 3, 1898, a massive avalanche swept from a slope 2,500 feet above the Chilkoot Trail. Within seconds the trail was buried under tons of snow, ice, rock and debris. Hundreds raced to dig for survivors. In total seventy men died. Other snow slides also took lives. Creeks could flash flood and take away a year's supplies in seconds. One flash flood drowned three men. The Chilkoot was a brutal, unrelenting pass, but it happened to be the best choice.

Pages 22-25: The final push to the Chilkoot summit is a thirty-degree slope called the "Golden Stair." In all seasons, snow slopes and steep ice cover this rocky gain. The Golden Stair had fifteen hundred steps cut into it, with a single icy rope to clutch to. Once a man stepped out of line, it could take him several hours to rejoin the trudge up the mountain.

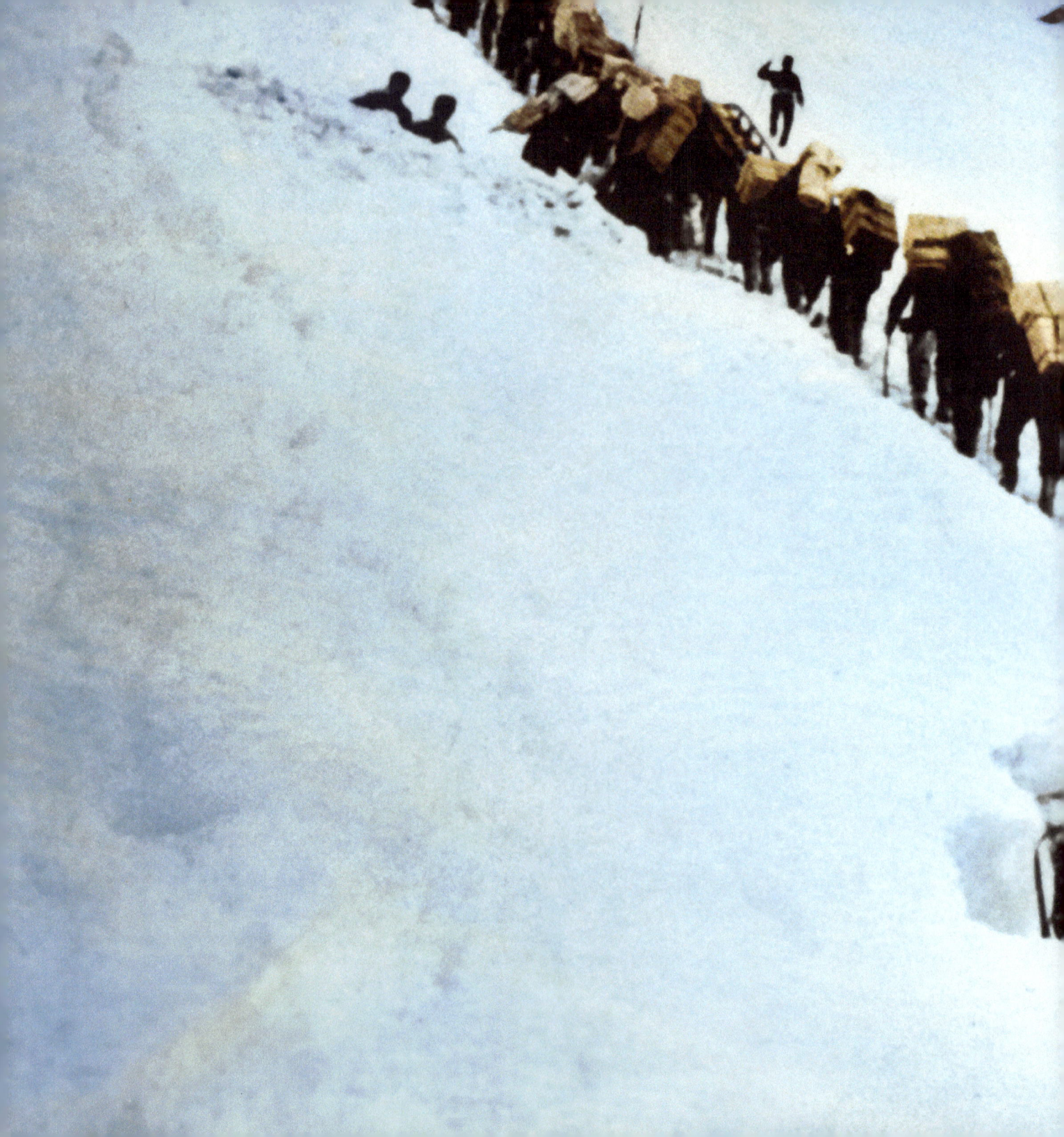

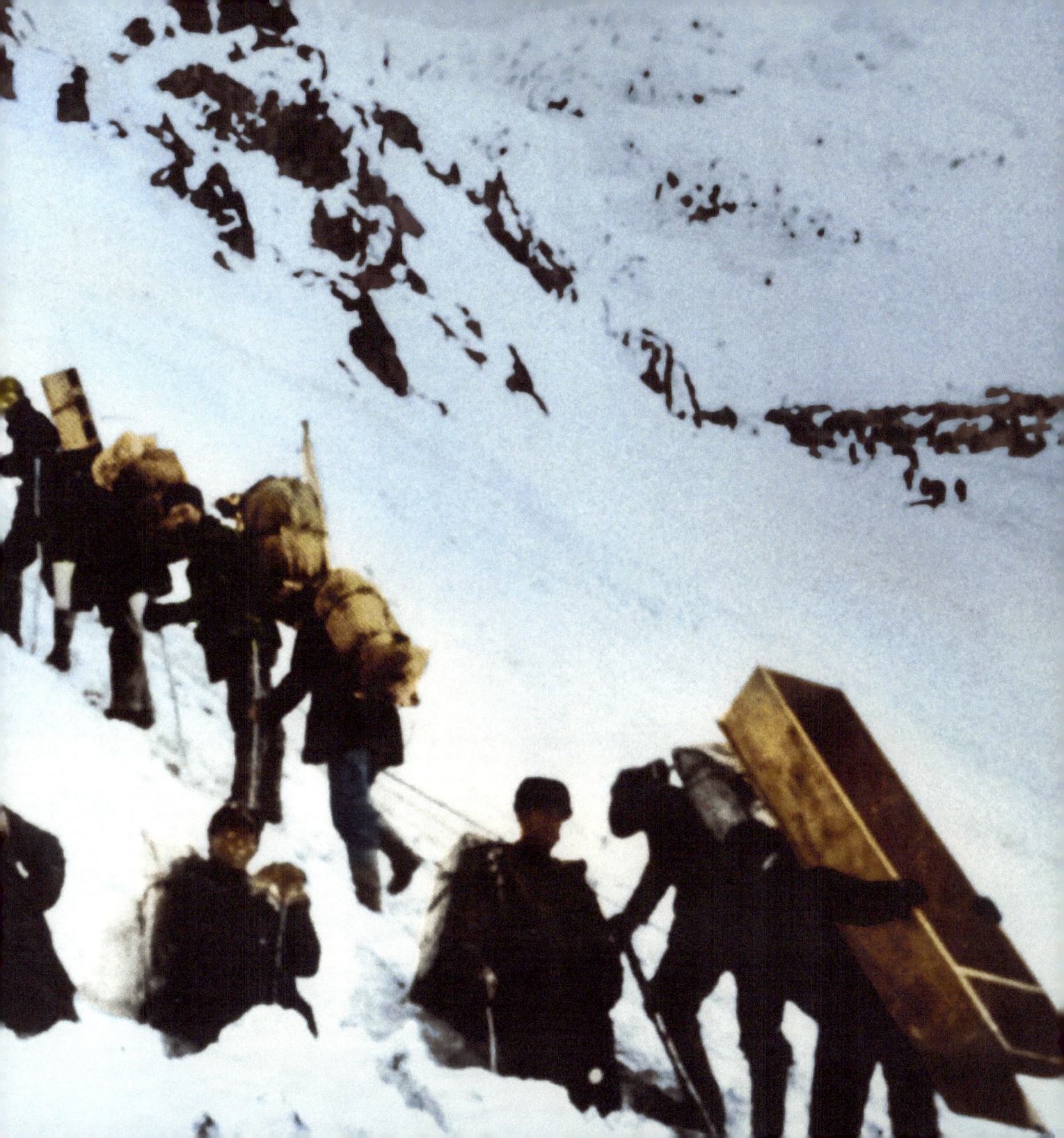

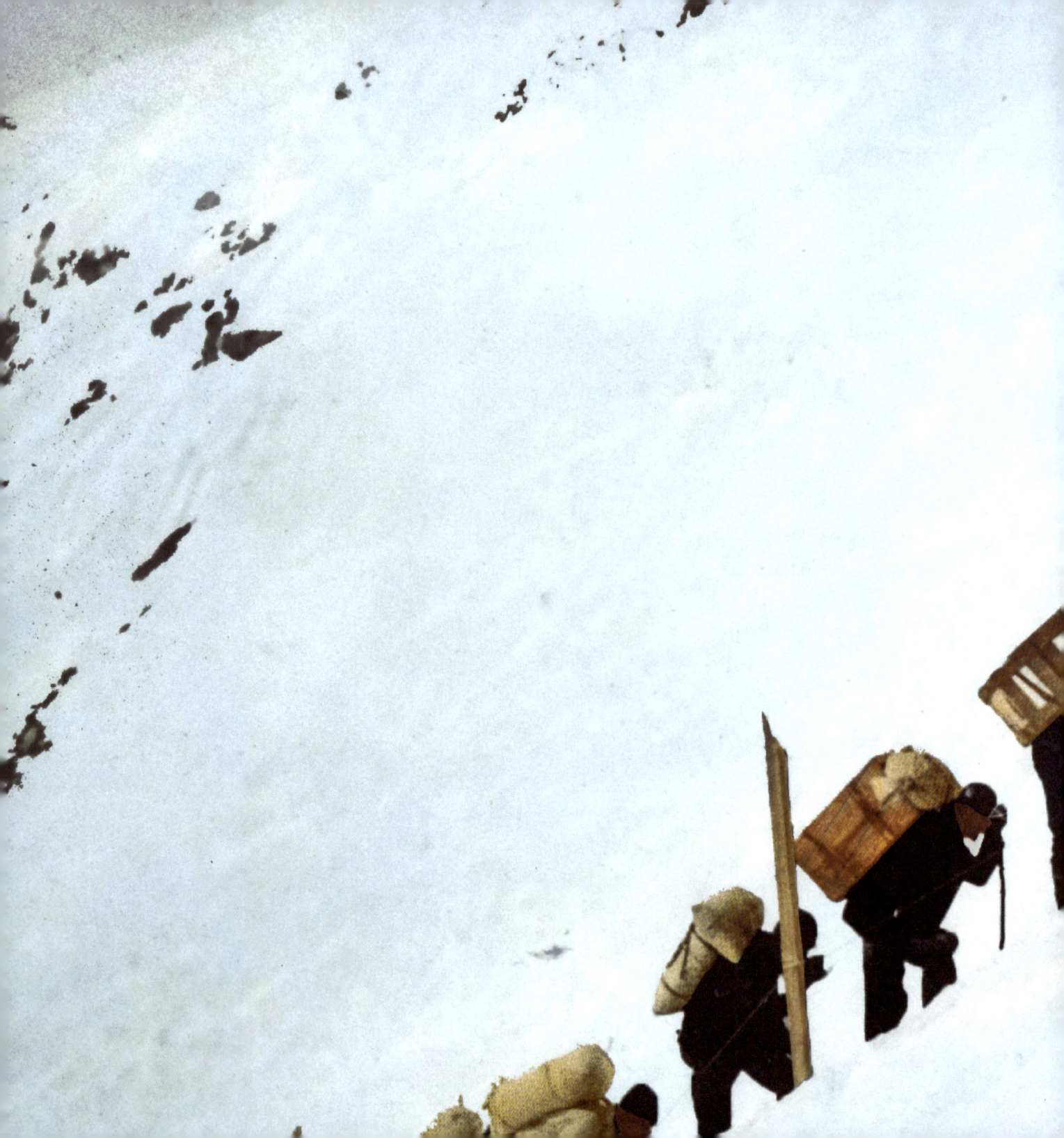

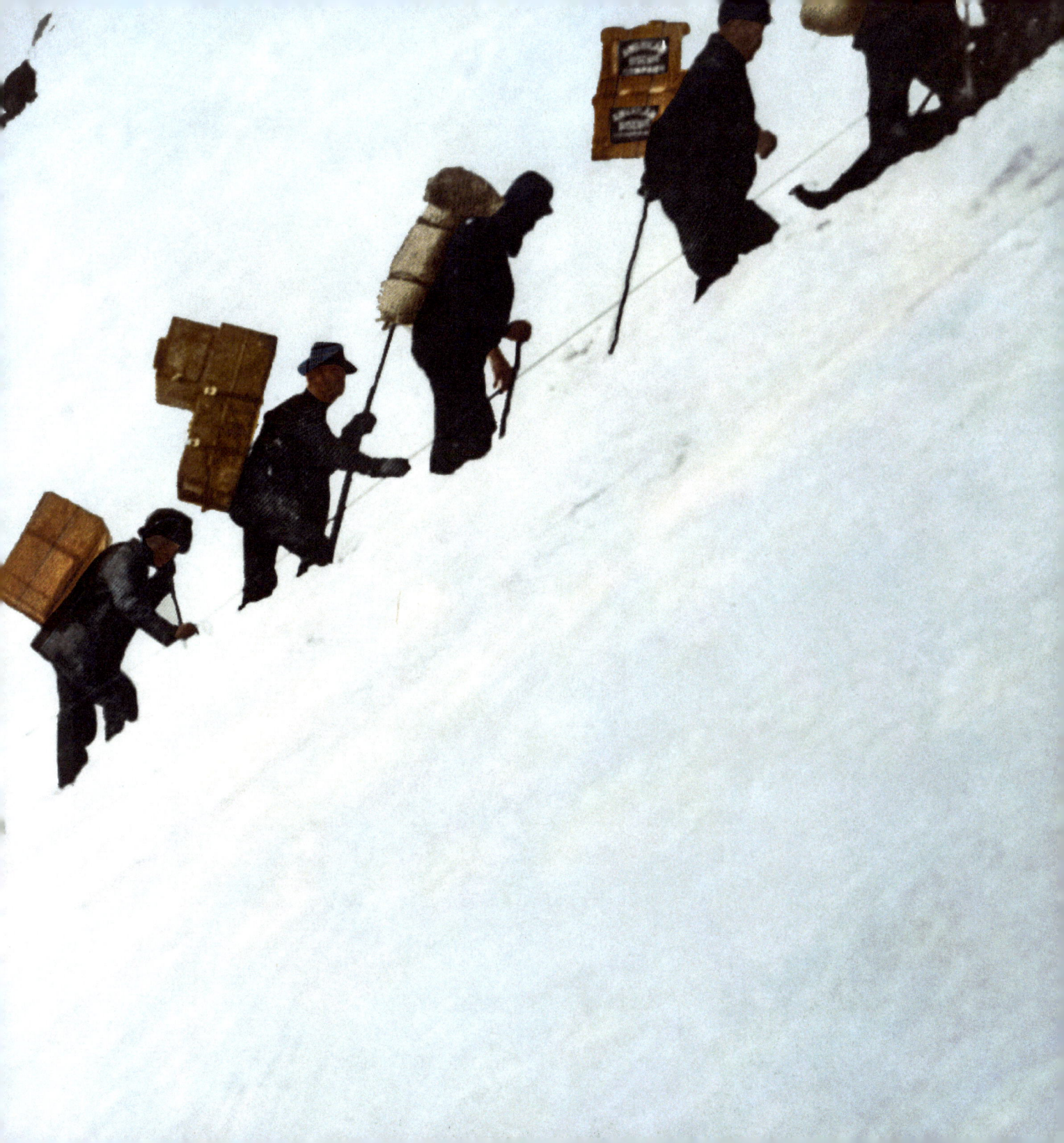

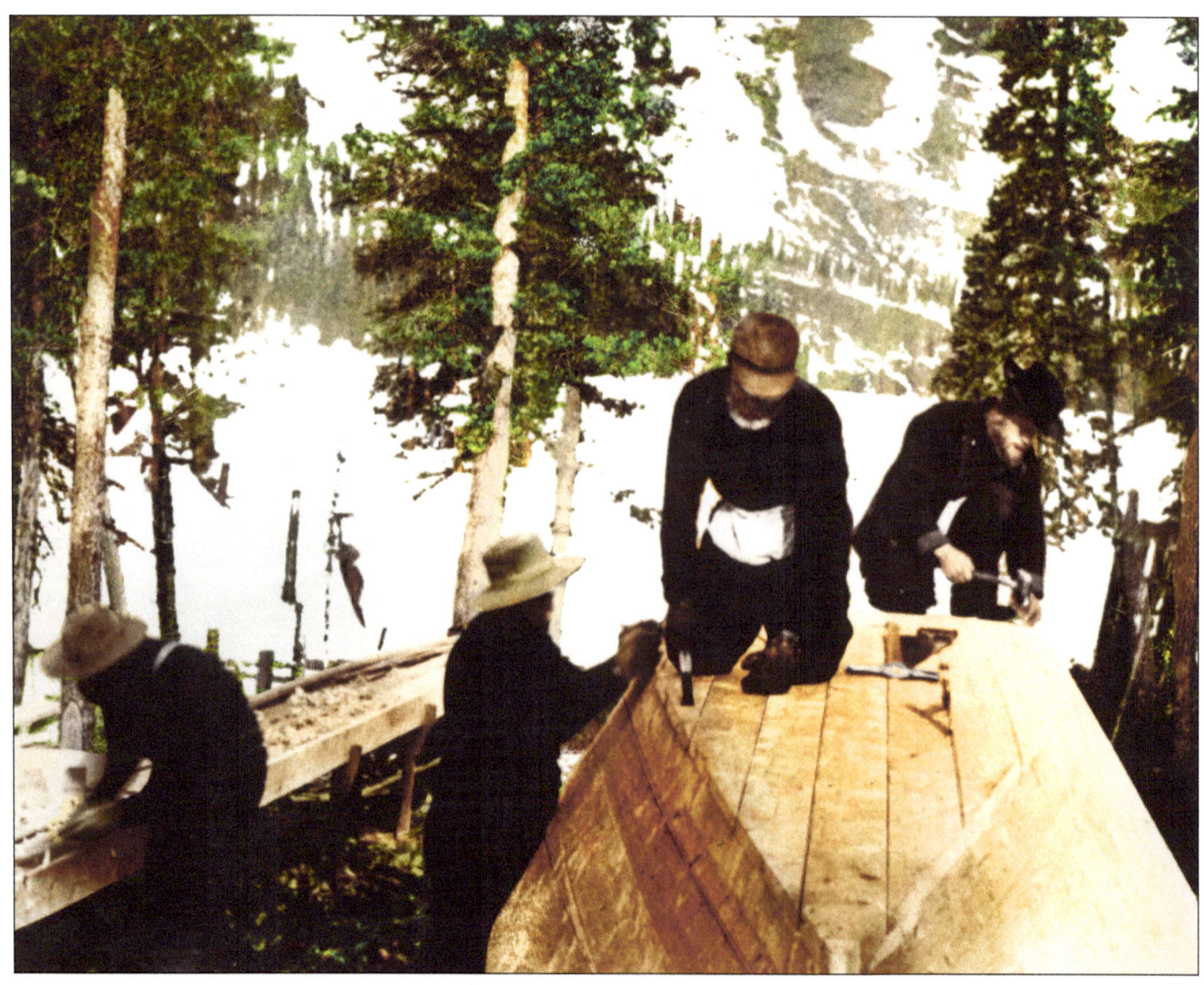

Above: Once over the Chilkoot Pass, the Stampeders were still a long way from the gold fields. After spring break-up they paddled and sailed through a series of lakes to reach the Yukon River. Flat-bottomed boats, as in this photograph, were commonly built due to their relative ease of construction.

Opposite: Boat-building towns were established on the rocky outcrops surrounding Lakes Lindeman and Bennett. During the winter of 1897-98 more than 20,000 people with little or no experience built 7,000 boats.

The landscape was stripped of its trees for firewood and planking for boats. The whipsawing of dimensioned lumber was the most onerous task of building these boats, and many parties split up as a result of fights in the saw pits. Once enough lumber was sawed, crude little boats were tacked together. The sound of hammers pounding oakum to seal boat hulls filled the valley.

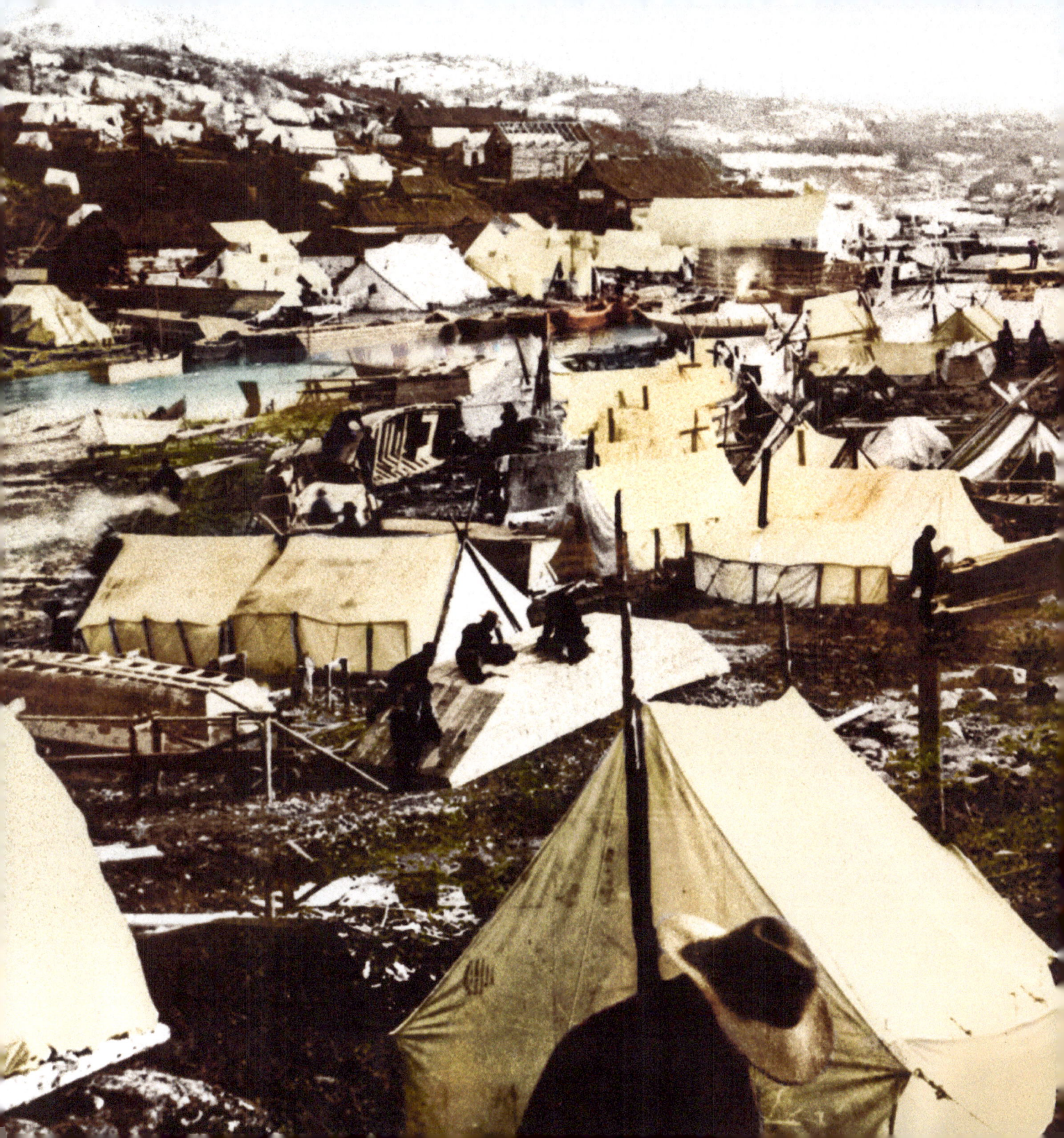

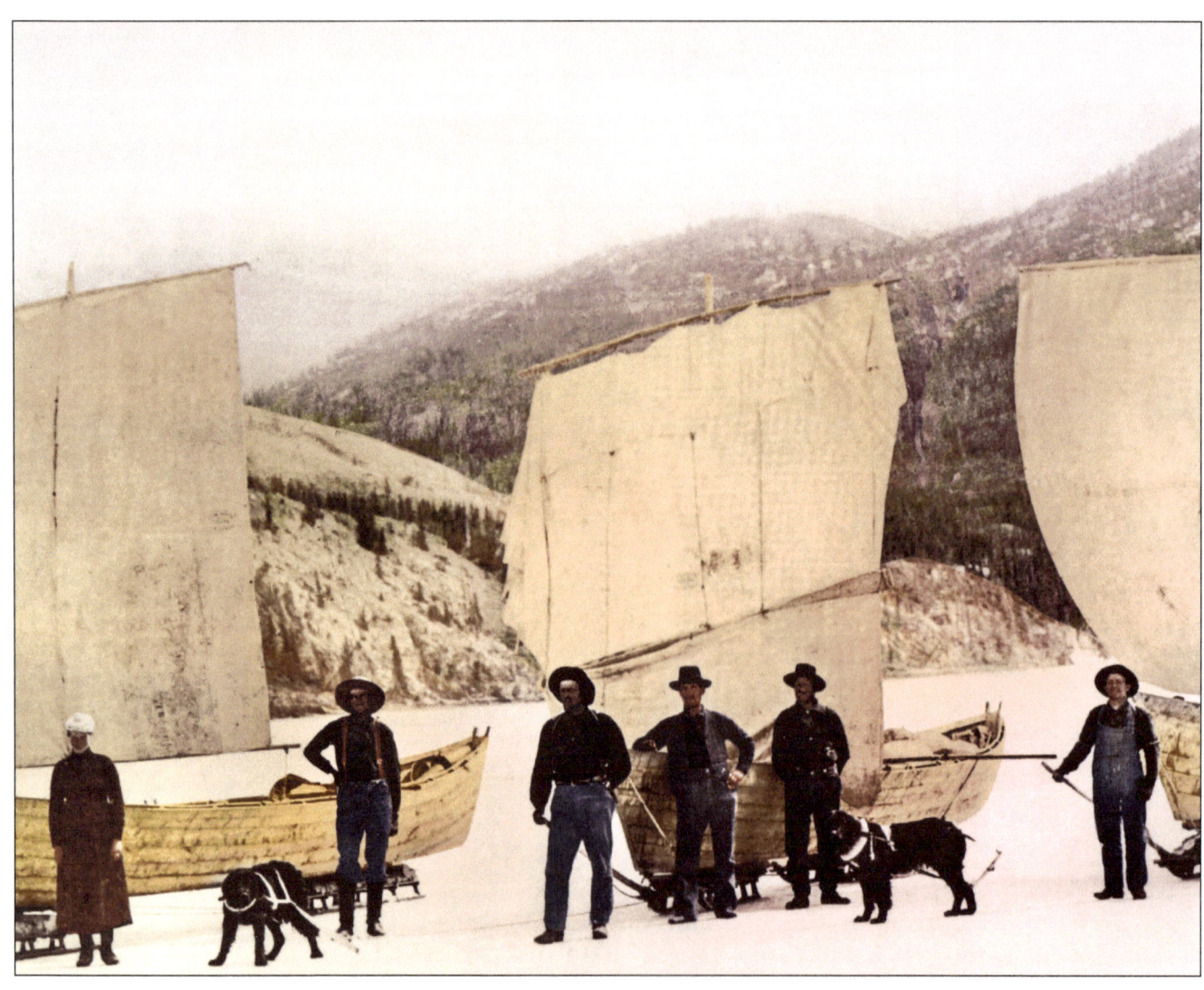

Above: Eager Stampeders on ice-covered Lake Bennett with sails attached to their supply-laden sleds and boats and rope harnesses over their shoulders for towing. The lakes close to the Chilkoot were at higher elevation and thawed later and these efforts could get these Stampeders downriver earlier.

Opposite: On June 3, 1898, the ice finally went out, and the most rickety armada ever seen set off for Dawson. The progress on the frequently windy and choppy lakes slowed many, but once on the Yukon River a swift current made up for lost time.

Pages 30 and 31: Men pulling a boat by rope from shore while the men in the boat help with poles on Windy Arm, Tagish Lake. Other Stampeders' boats are barely visible on the lake.

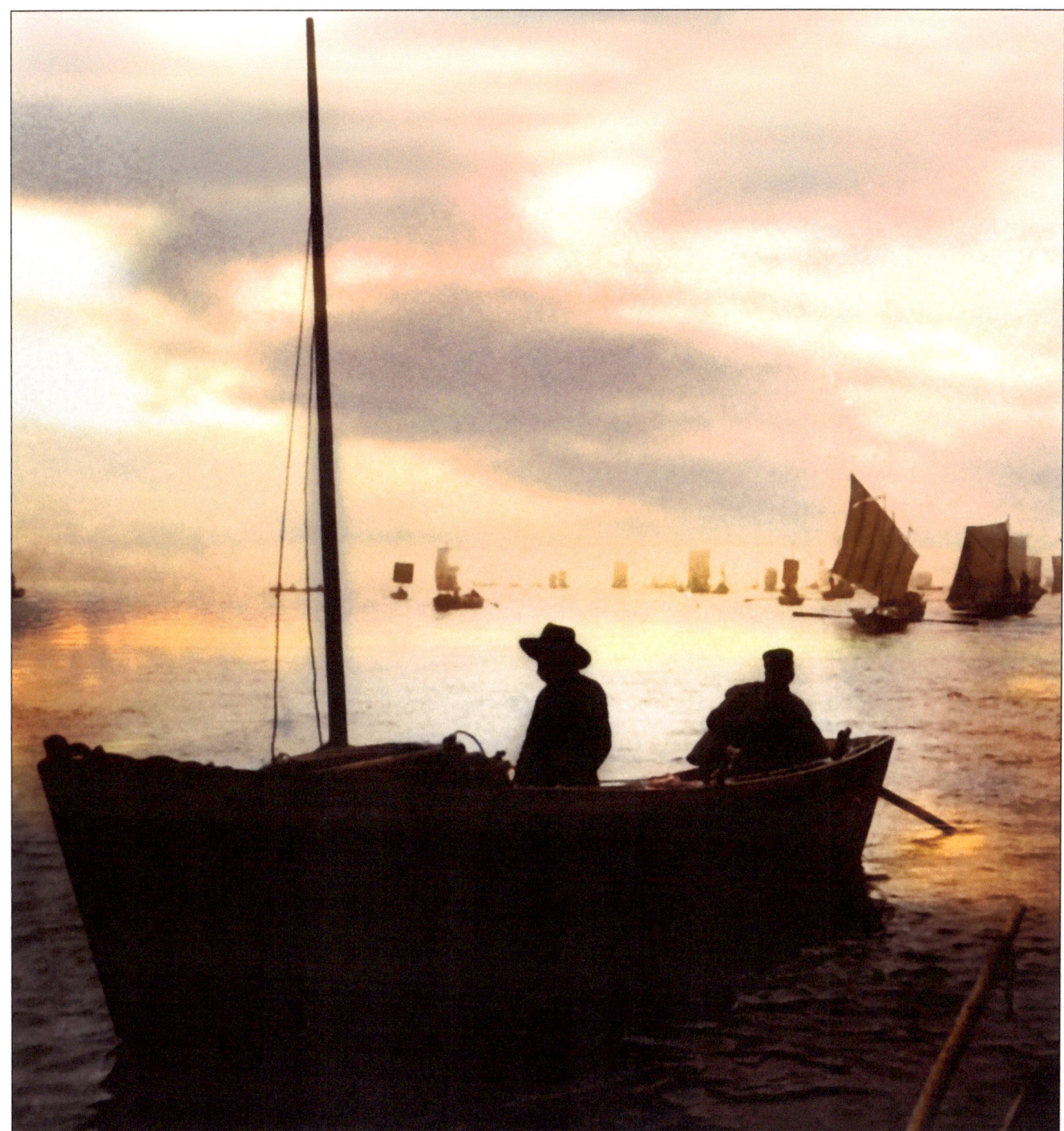

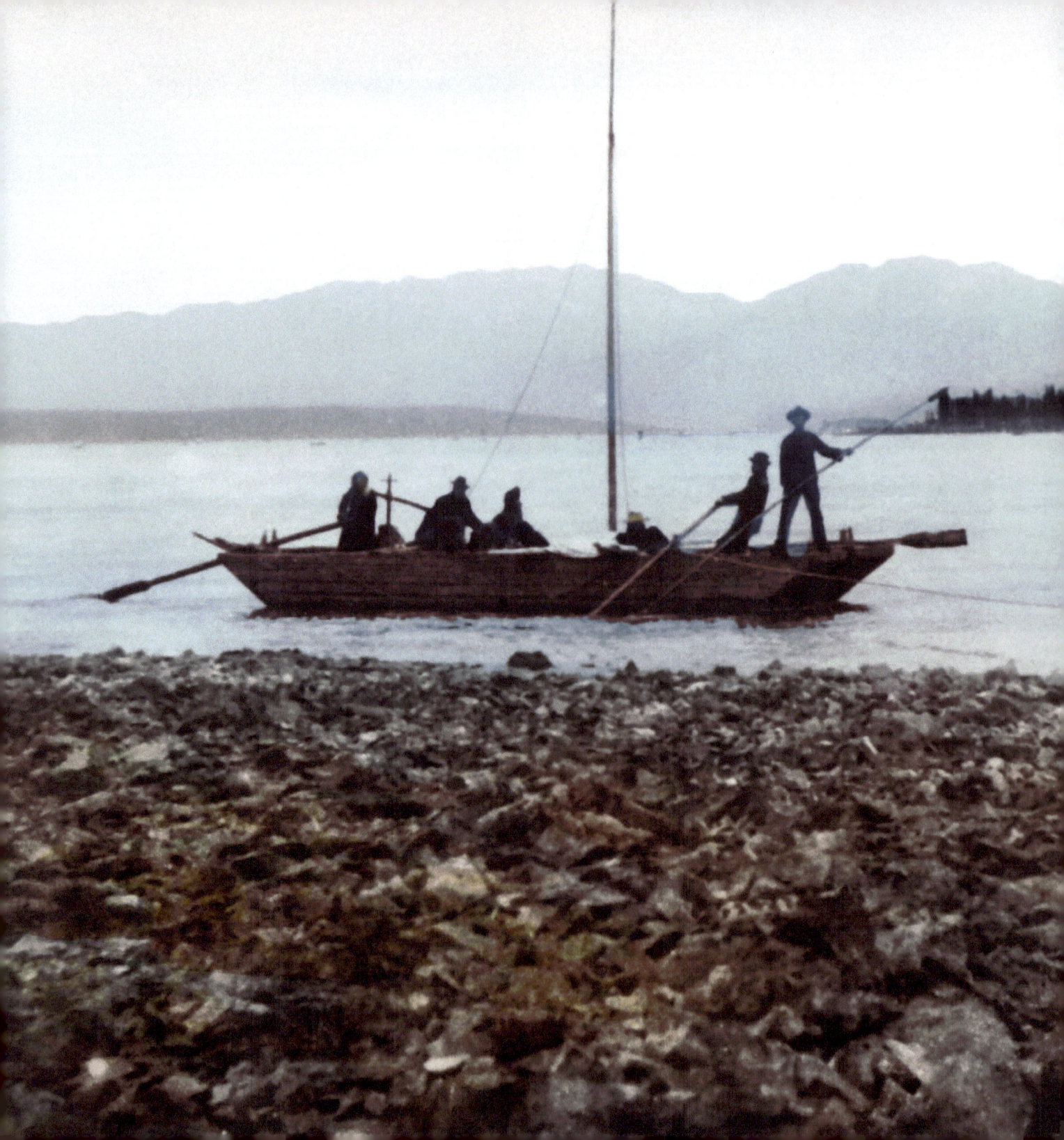

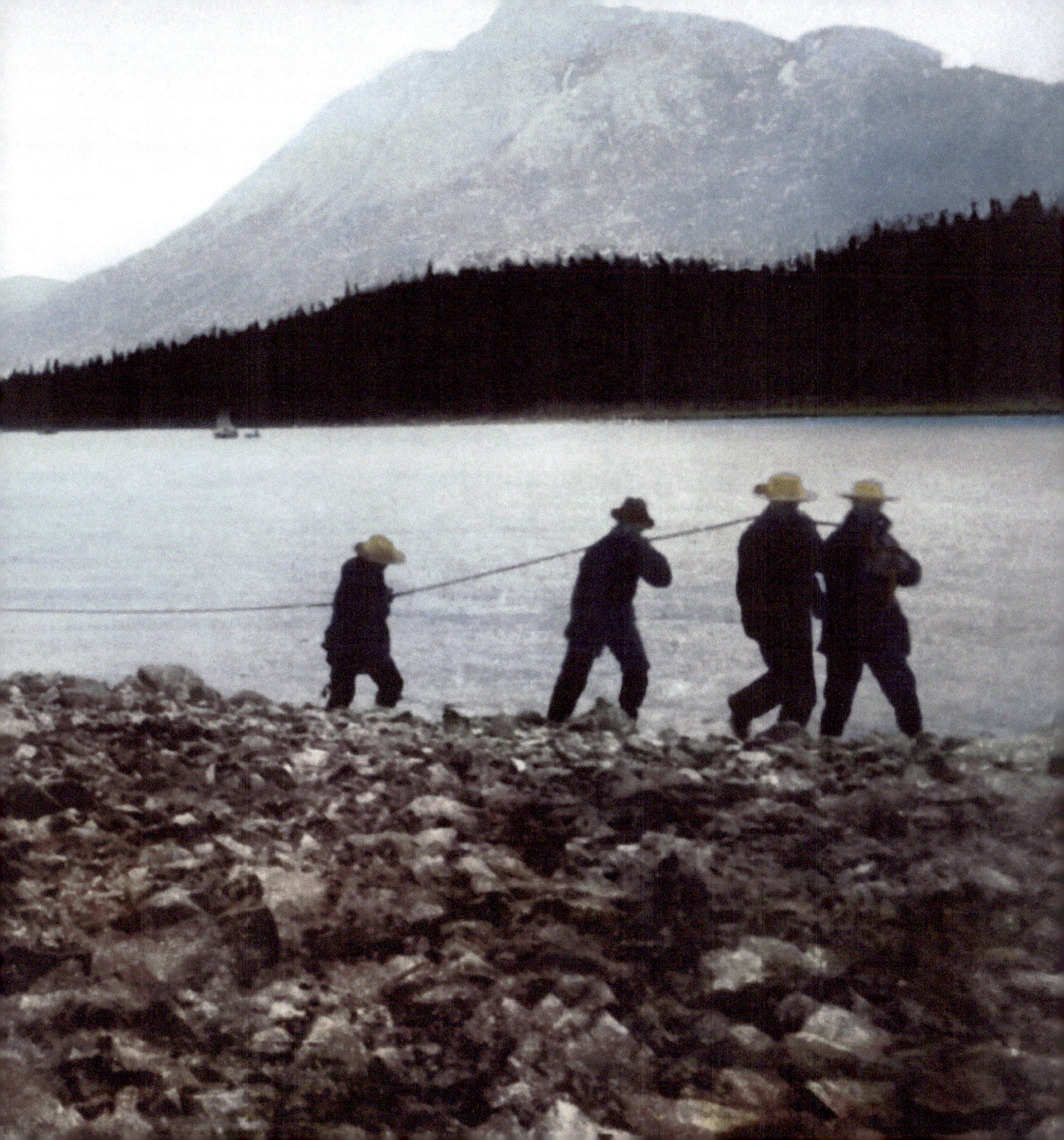

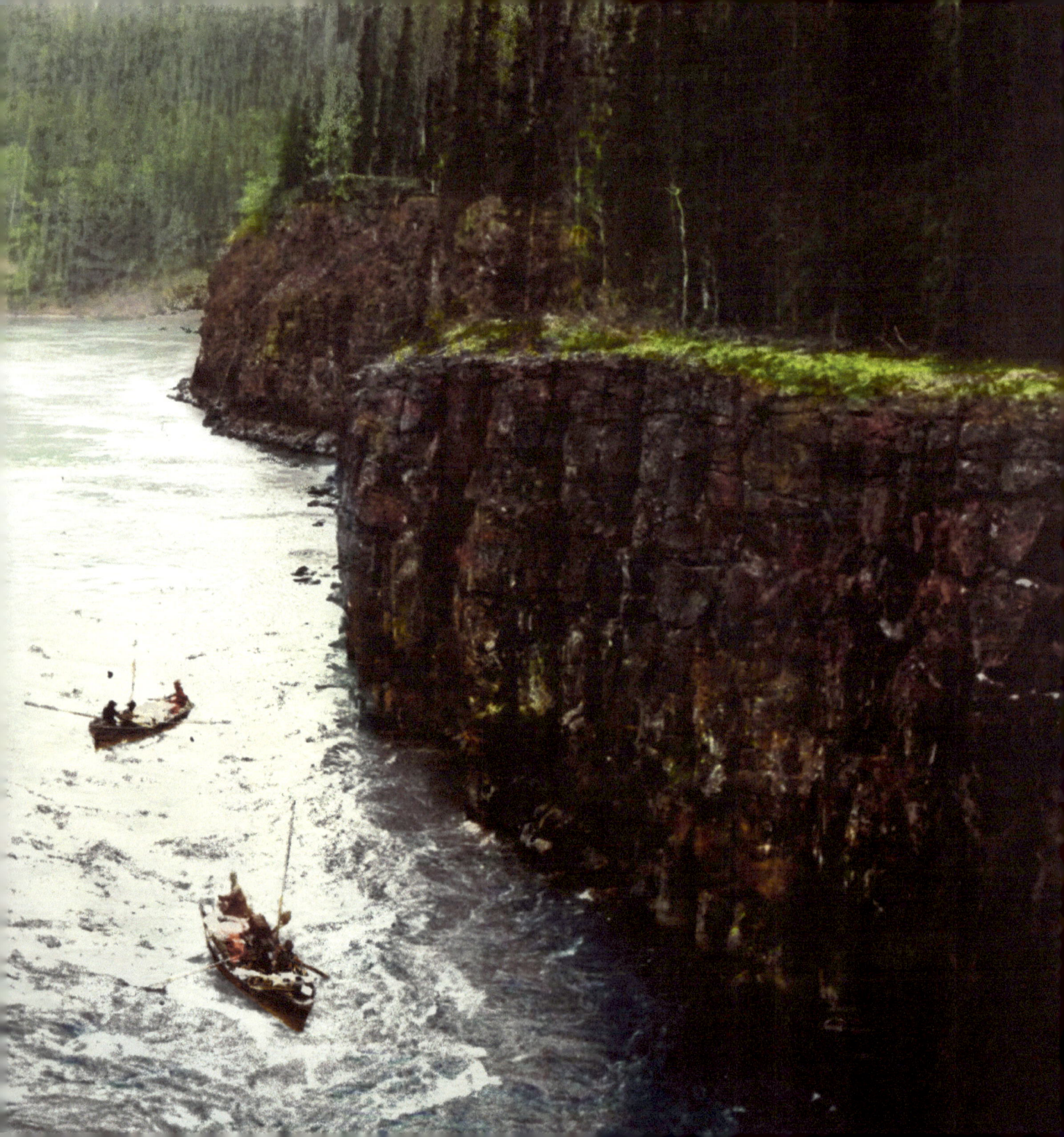

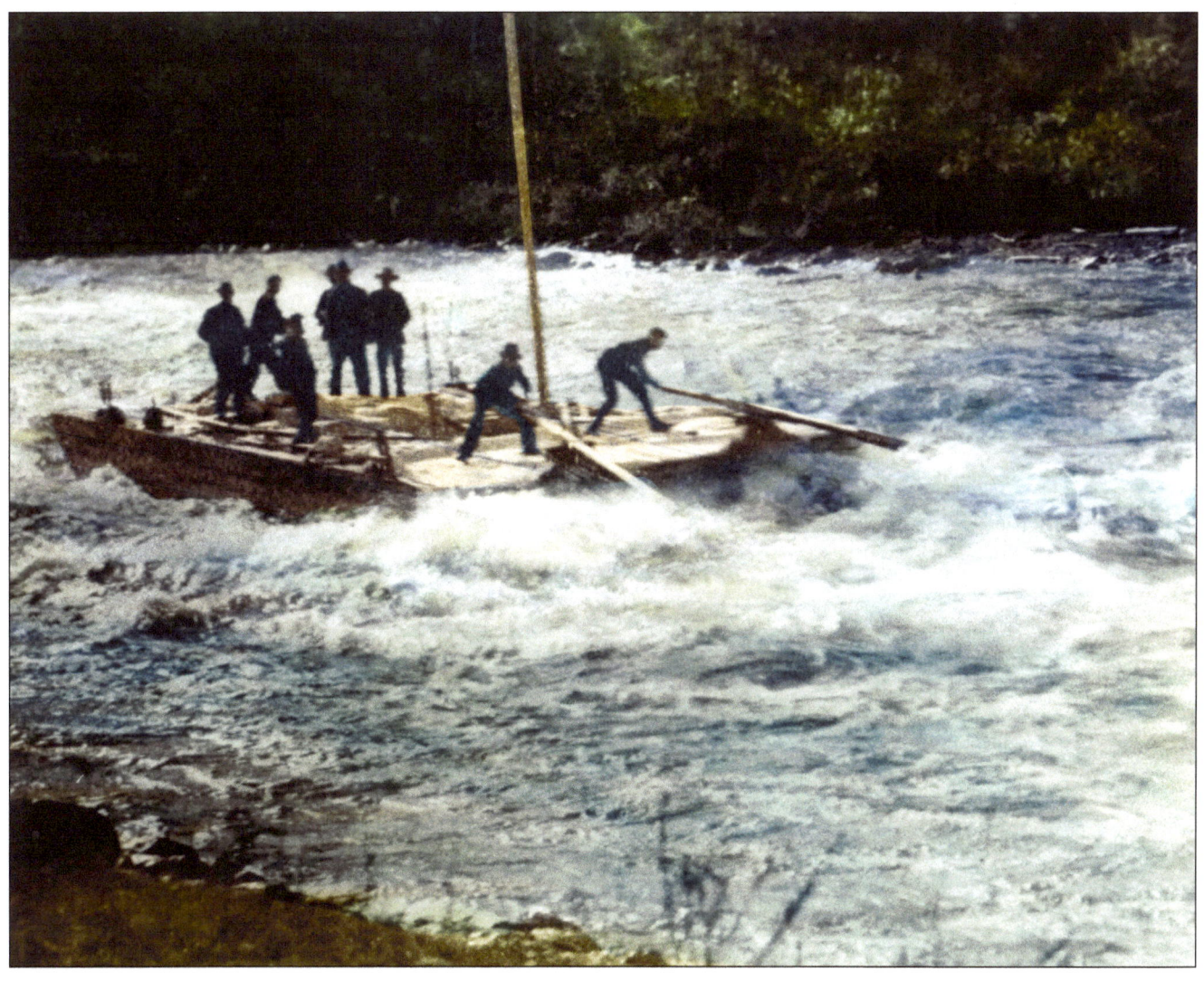

Above: A scow manned by eight men shooting Whitehorse Rapids. The two men on the bow are steering with oars.

Opposite: Stampeders running treacherous Miles Canyon, near Whitehorse. Stampeders tried to find a route through a long series of waves in the steep-walled canyon. In the week after break-up, more than 150 boats were destroyed and at least ten men drowned. A short time later a log tramline was built to haul boats and gear around this rapid. River guides also offered their services, and many of these guides were credited with hundreds of safe passages.

The remainder of the trip down the Yukon River was less difficult, though white water such as Five Finger Rapids deserved caution. The race to the Klondike was on, and in the midnight sun the Stampeders paddled around the clock.

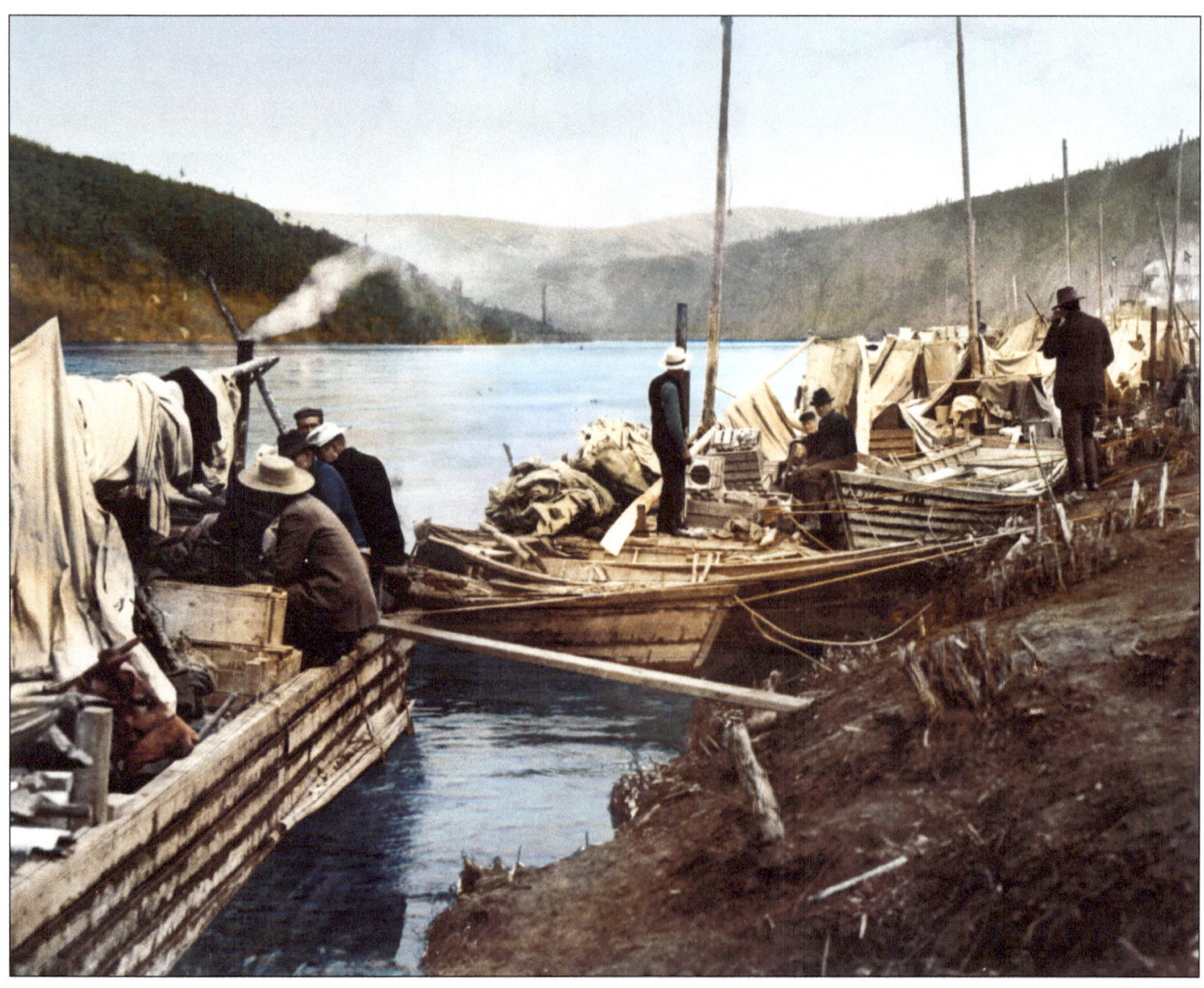

Above: Boats and barges line the shore of the Yukon River at Dawson. It was a true boom town with a heyday that lasted only a year or two. At its zenith Dawson had a population of more than 40,000 and was the largest Canadian city west of Winnipeg.

Most Stampeders arrived in Dawson in the spring and summer of 1898. They wandered into this carnival-like town exhausted from their arduous trek. There are many stories of Stampeders who upon arriving in Dawson immediately booked passage home, so travel weary and worn-out they did not even try to pan for gold.

Opposite: "Bowery Street" was the name given to the area along the Yukon River inhabited by tent dwellers. Merchants have their wares displayed under canvas awnings and in tents. Two emaciated horses can be seen at the bottom.

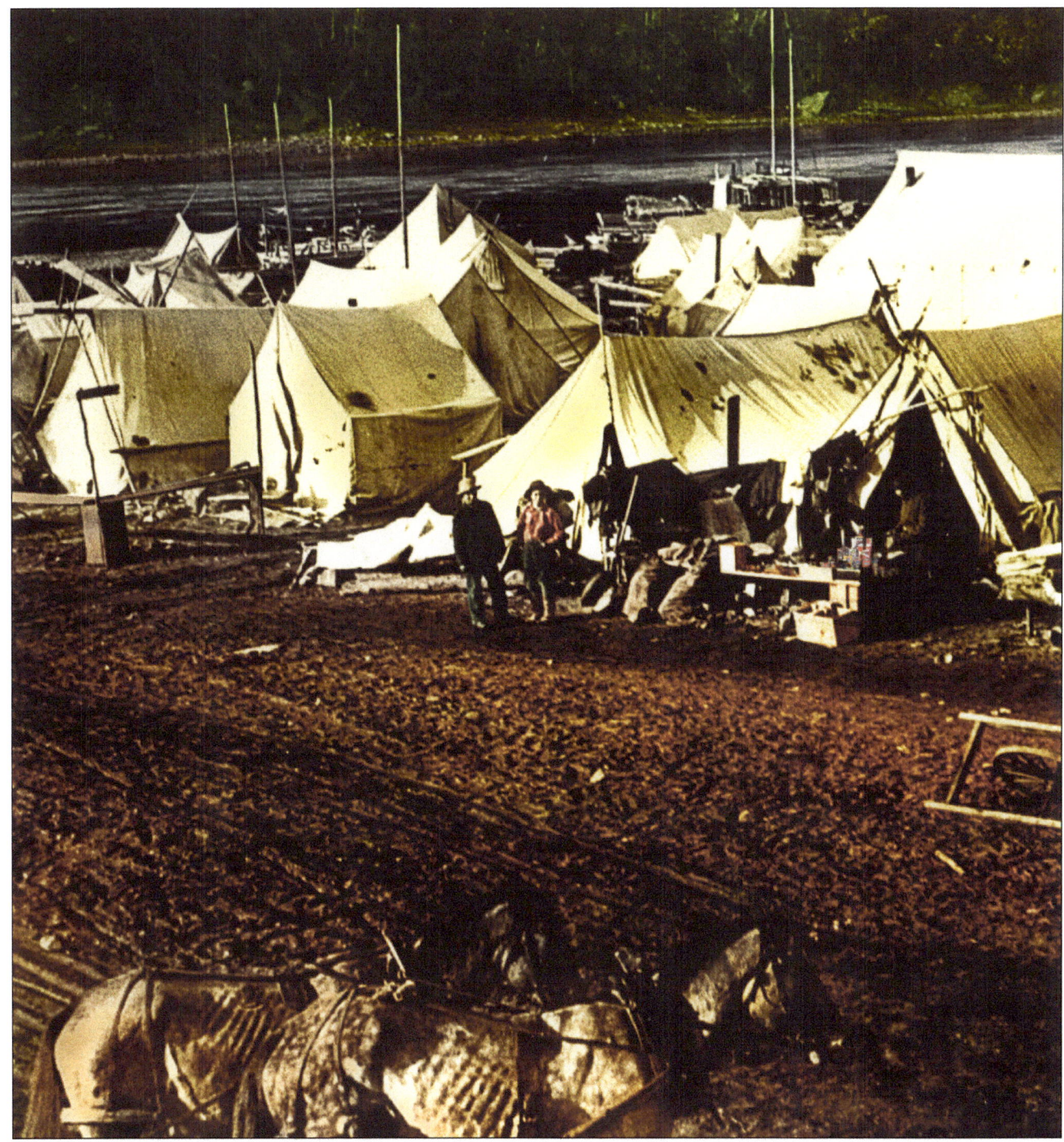

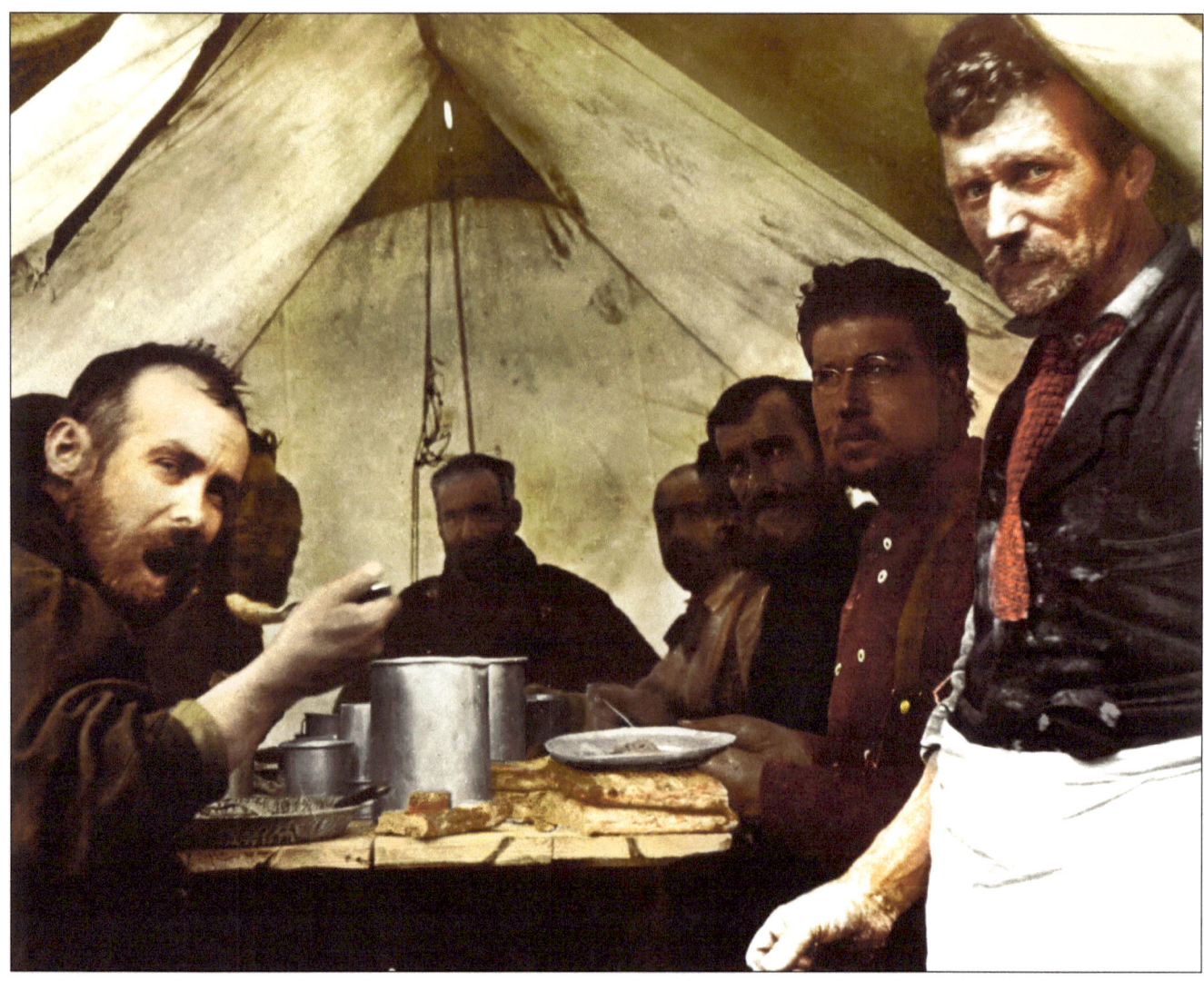

Above: Meals tended to be simple and repetitious for most Stampeders. Tent restaurants were popular as they were usually more affordable.

Most of the population of Dawson dined on beans and pancakes. They slept in canvas tents and spent their days in idle anticipation of finding their fortune. They had endured the most arduous and difficult experience of their life just getting to the Klondike valley. Now they were idle with little opportunity to stake or even work someone's claim.

Opposite: Horse and cart stuck in the mud on Second Avenue. Dawson was built on a swamp, and after a hard rain some of its streets became impassable. The puddles were an ideal habitat for mosquitos and flies and human and animal waste created a terrible stench. Diseases like typhoid flourished under these conditions.

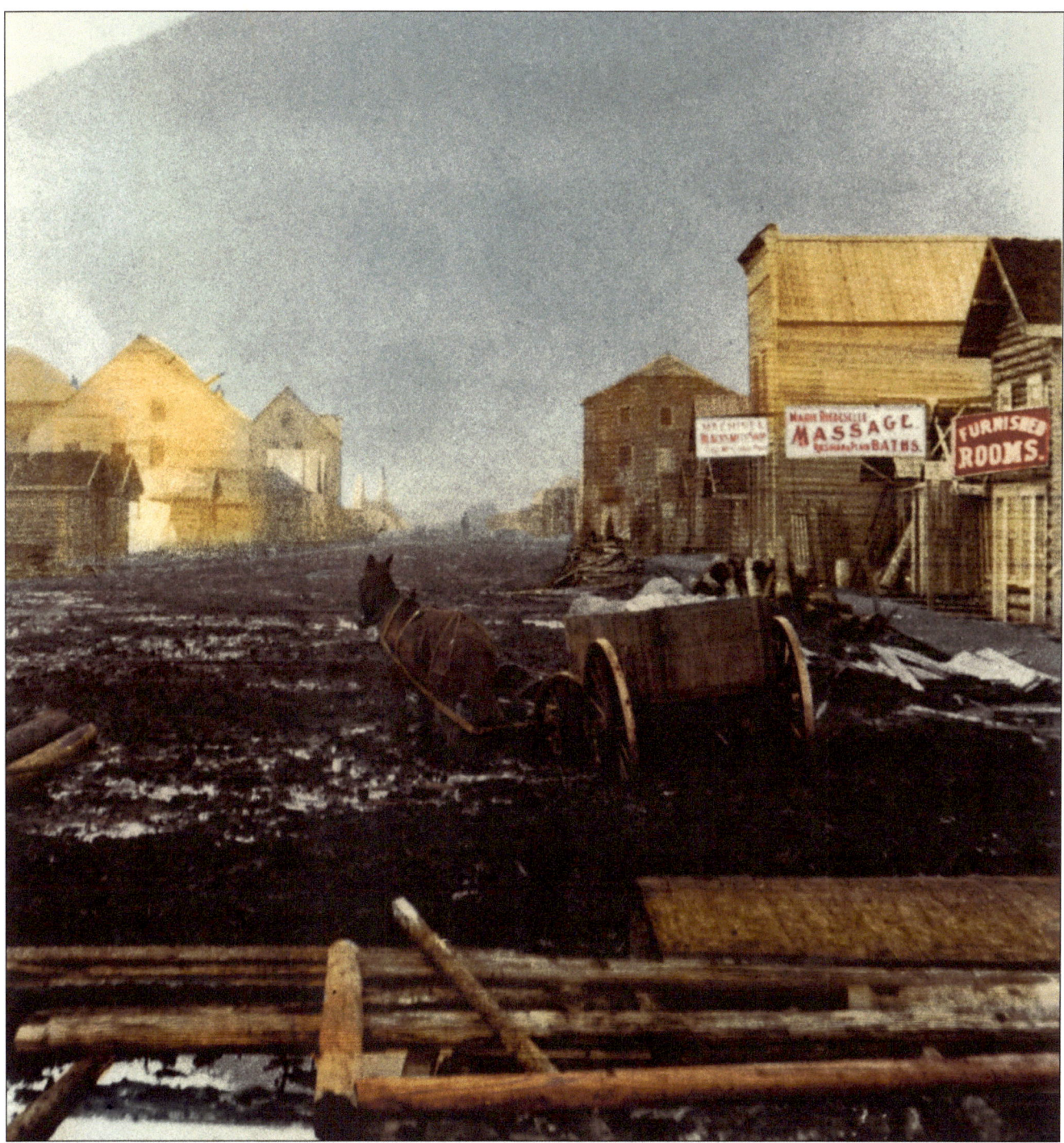

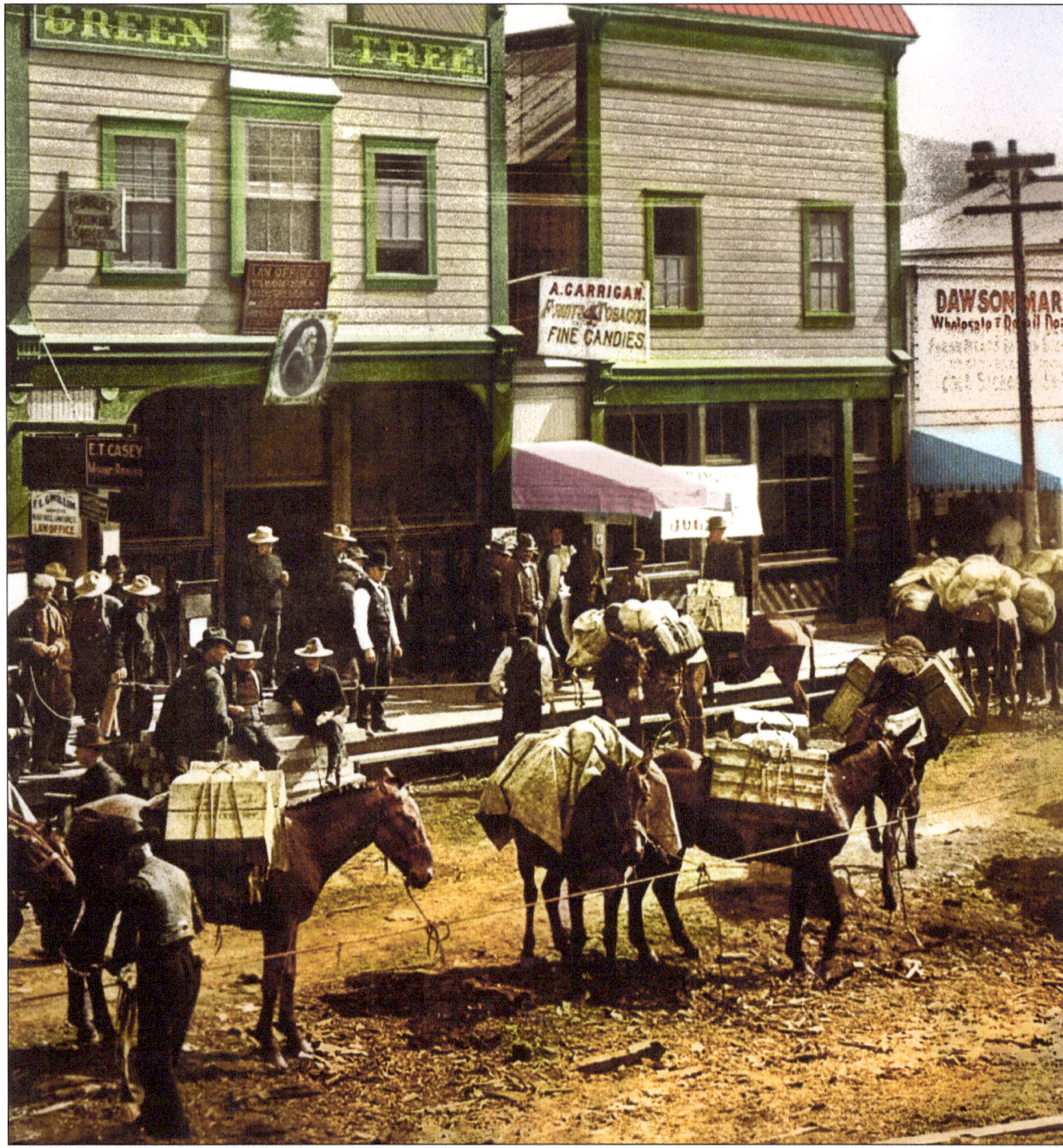

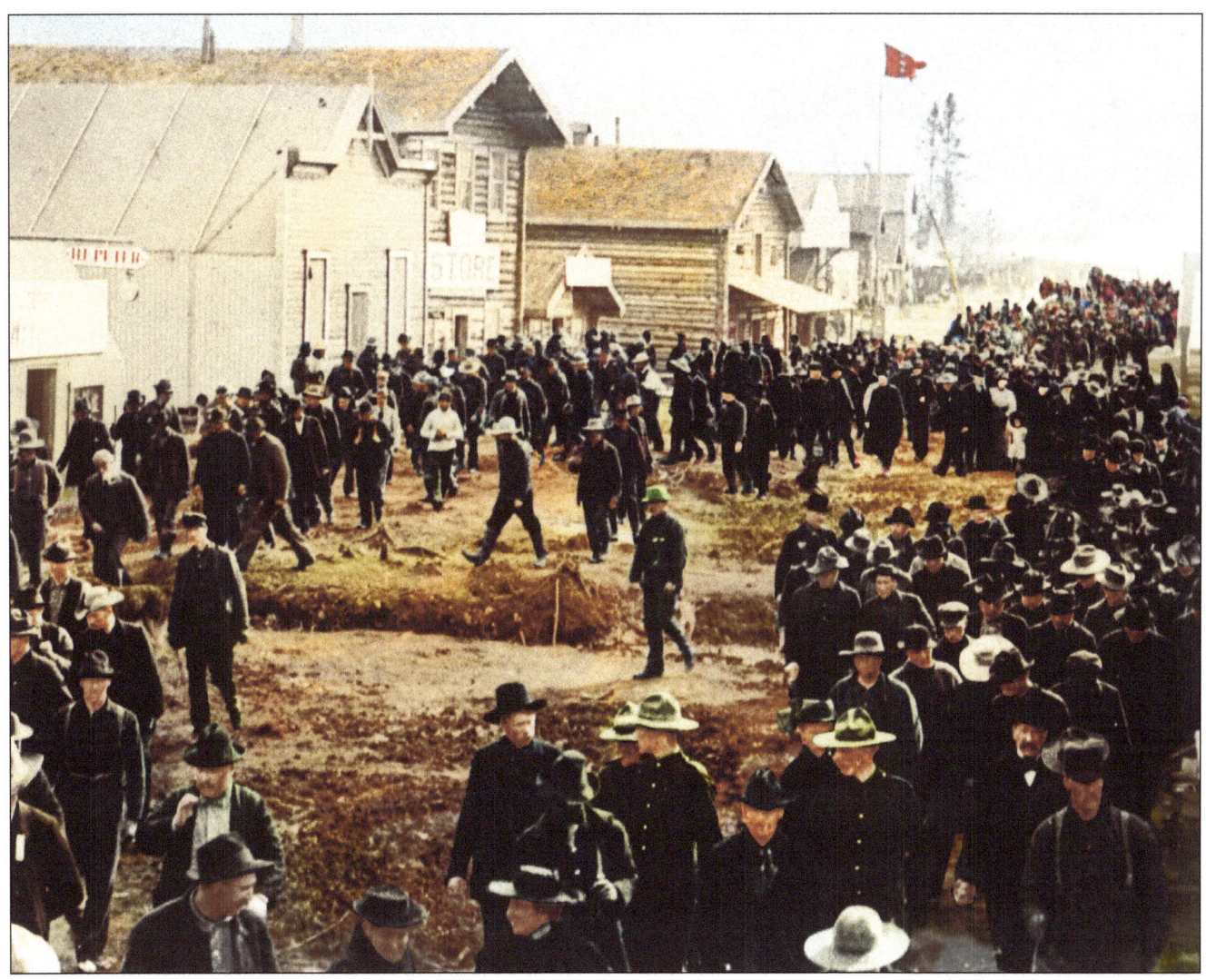

Above: July 4th celebrations of U.S. Independence Day were observed in Dawson. More than sixty percent of Stampeders were U.S. citizens.

The irony of the Klondike Gold Rush was that the gold fields had been almost entirely staked the year before the Stampeders arrived. There was little opportunity for day laborers and many Stampeders were flat broke. Dawson was a boom town where the fabulously rich and the dirt poor walked the same wooden planks over the marshy streets. Despair was everywhere except in the dance halls, saloons and shops.

Opposite: Pack trains were commonly used to haul supplies around town and to the mines at the nearby creeks.

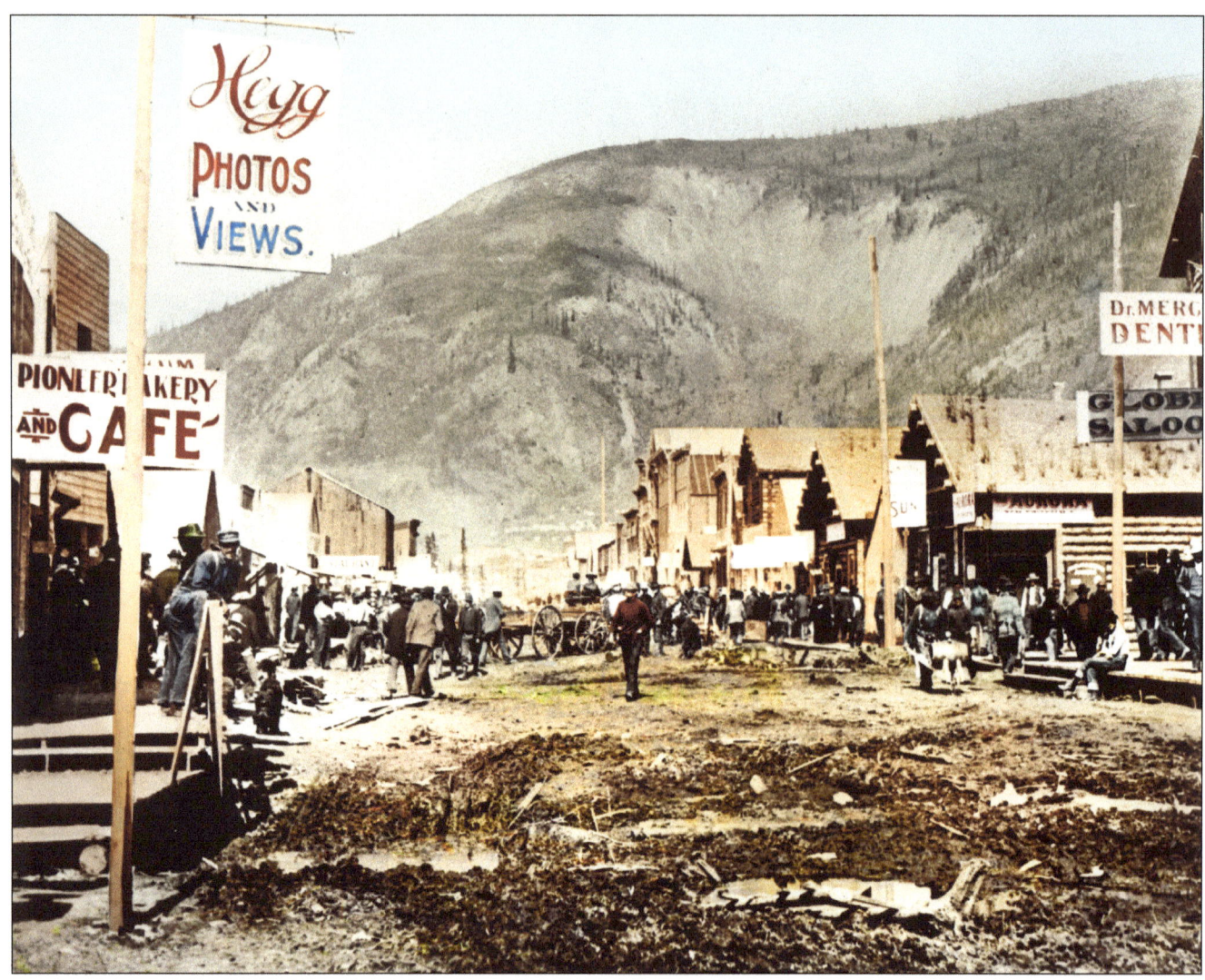

Above: Front Street was the center of town. Hastily built hotels, restaurants and warehouses lined the streets. The landslide above Dawson City appears much the same today and this hill is known as the "Dome."

For a brief moment Dawson was the "Paris of the North" and had a range of goods and services that haven't been seen since. In Dawson you could buy the best champagne and sip it in fine crystal. You could dine on filet mignon, oysters and caviar. Fine silks, jewelry and gowns were available for a price. Virtually anything was possible in Dawson.

Opposite: Receiving mail was an event for a city filled with homesick Stampeders. During the winter the mail was carried by dog teams and later by horse-drawn sleighs. Paddlewheelers kept the town stocked and carried the mail during the summer months.

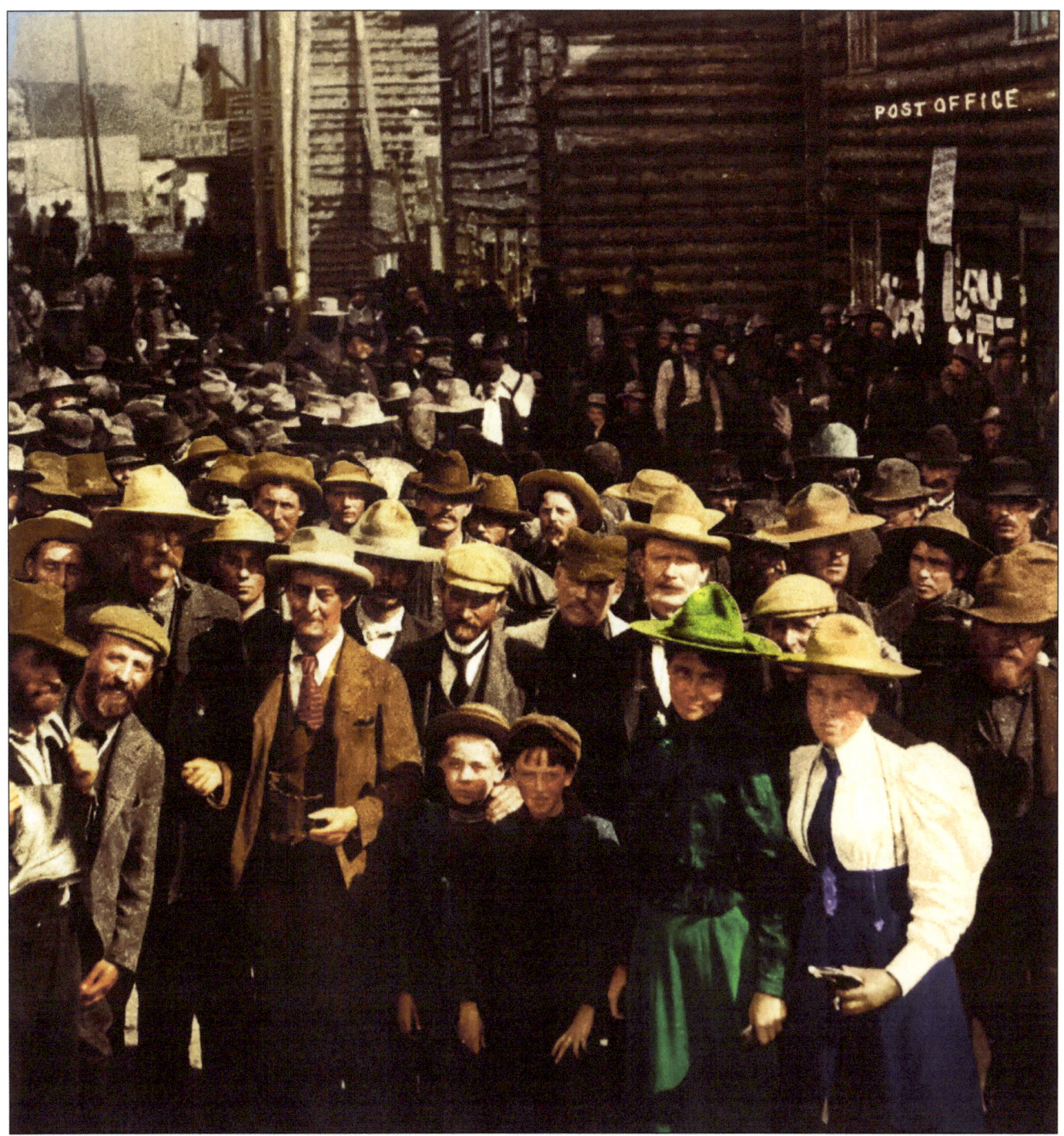

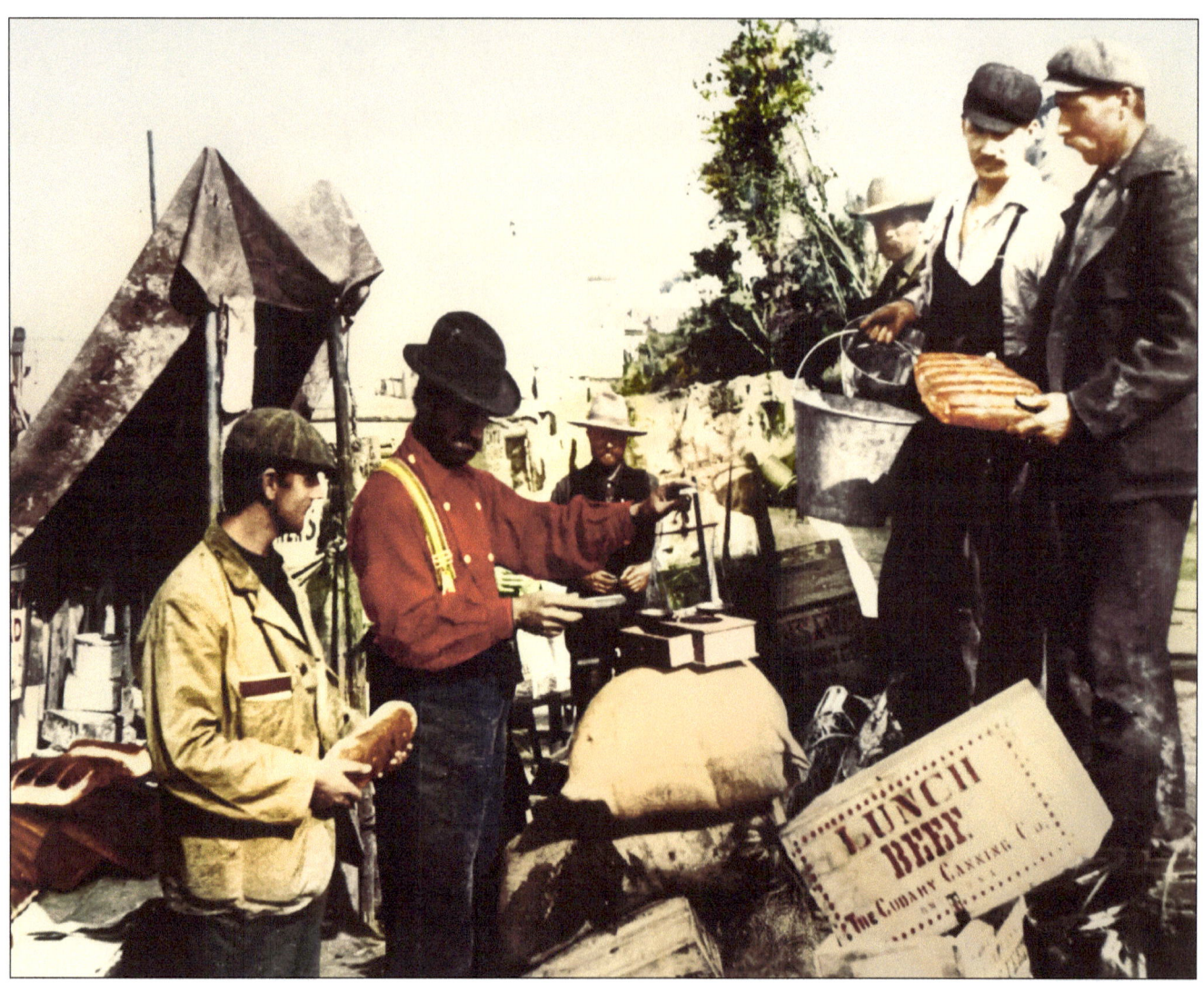

Above: A baker exchanging gold dust for bread. Gold dust was an accepted currency in Dawson and most entrepreneurs had scales readily available.

Opposite: A tent store specializing in fresh lemonade. Stores like this could earn their proprietors a small fortune. Waffles were particularly popular in Dawson and many restaurants and street vendors served them. Many women became very successful through these sorts of ventures.

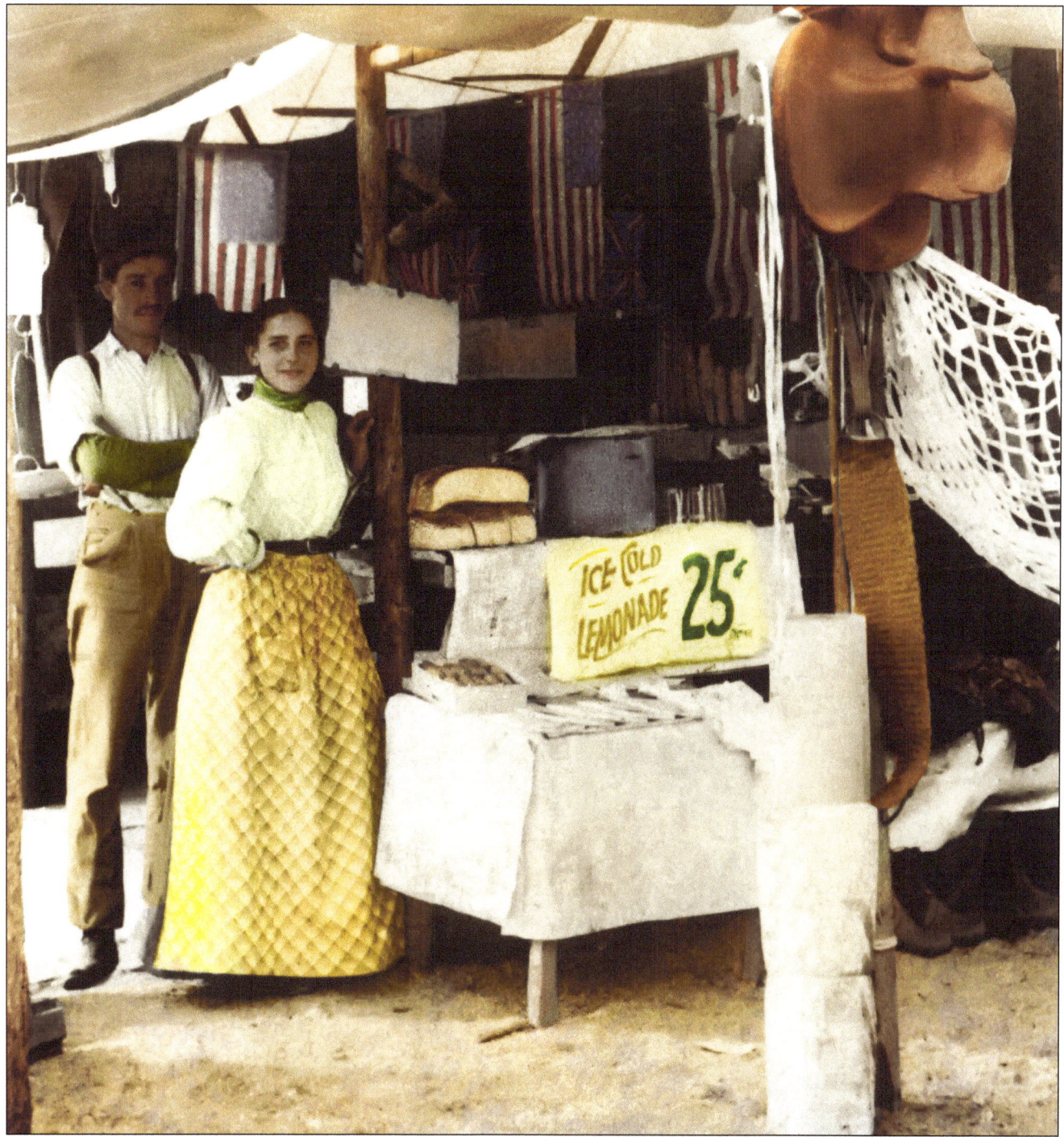

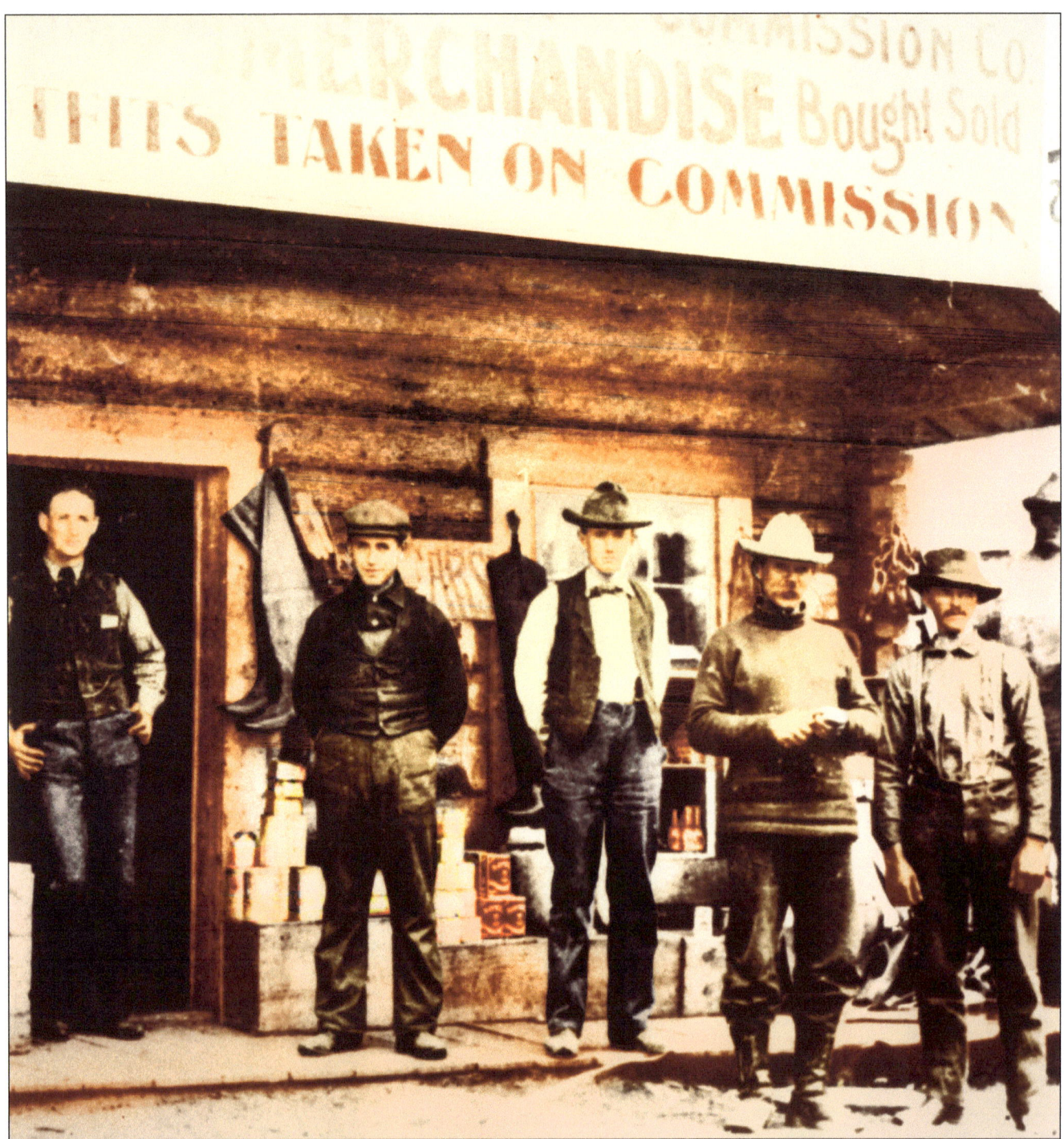

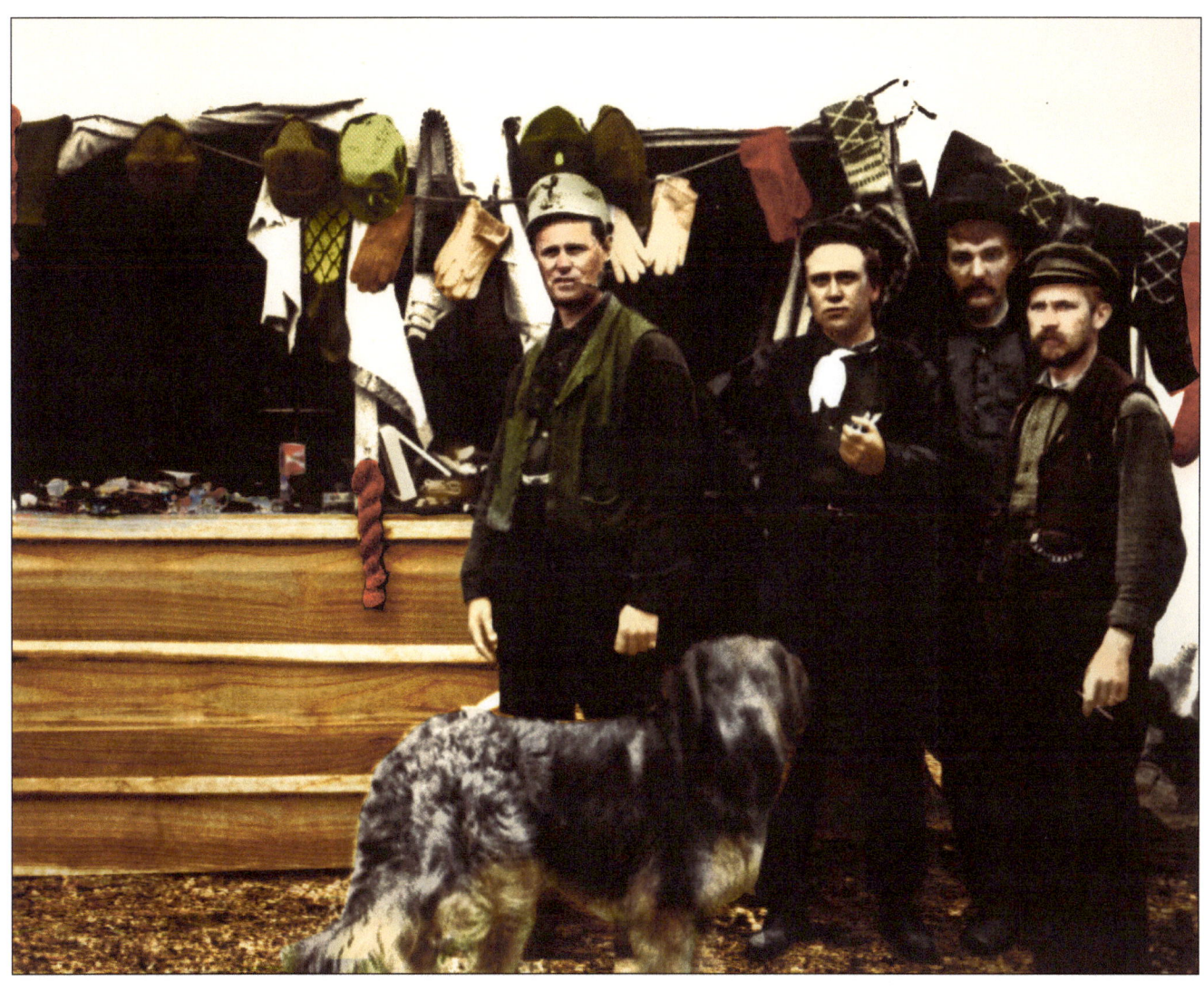

Above: Many stores were housed in tents, especially on Bowery Street. They often sold gear from Stampeders that returned home, though some enterprising merchants brought unique products to Dawson.

Opposite: Exterior of a general store that also sold the supplies and equipment of Stampeders who decided to return home.

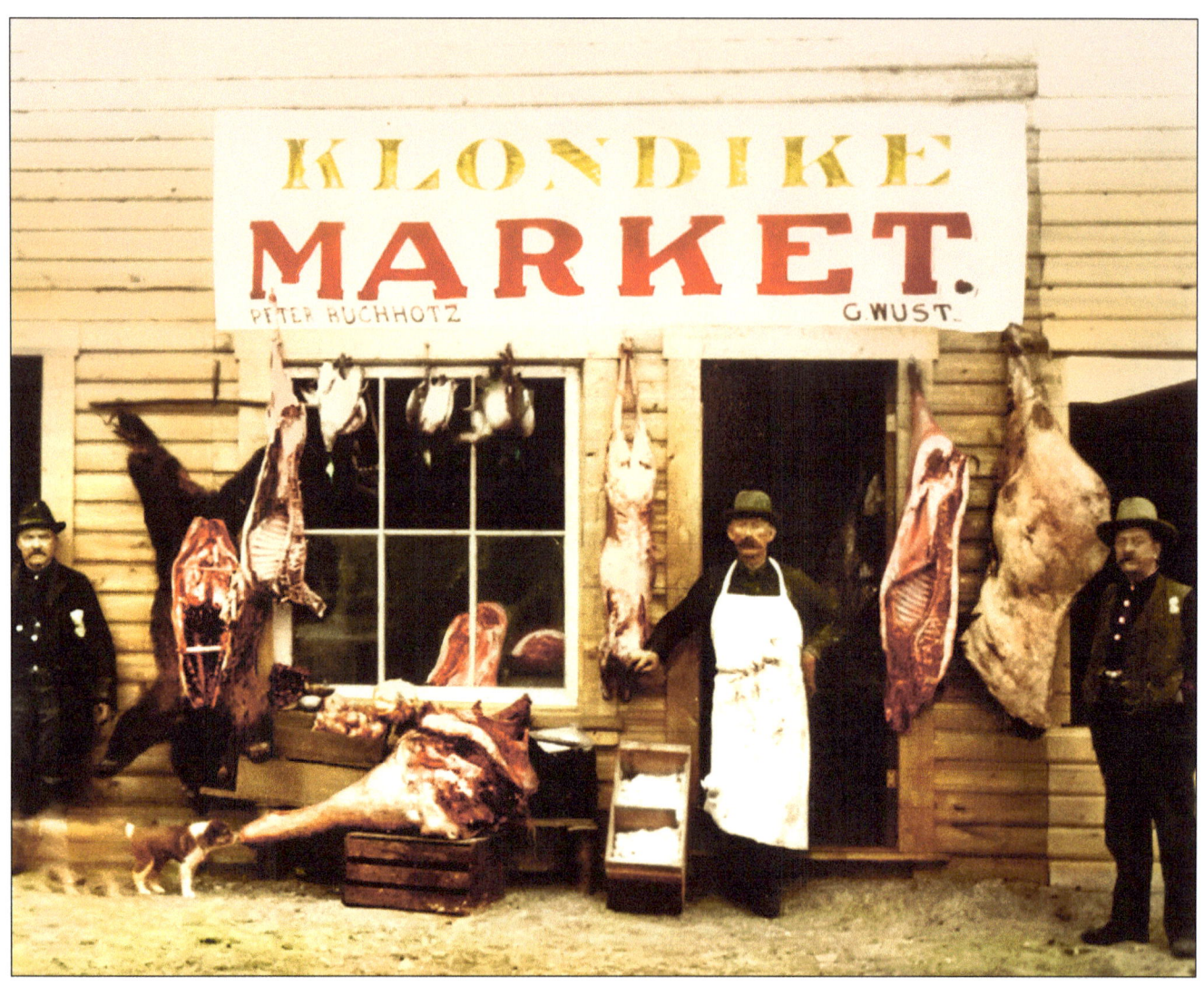

Above: A market selling wild meat, which is hung in front of the store. A slaughtered bear is prominent on the left. Local wildlife populations were decimated during the gold rush.

Opposite: Exterior of the popular Pacific Hotel. A St. Bernard dog sleeps in the street. Most hotels offered gambling which included poker, faro and roulette. Many saloons stayed open around the clock but the police made sure they closed on Sundays. The drink of choice was whiskey.

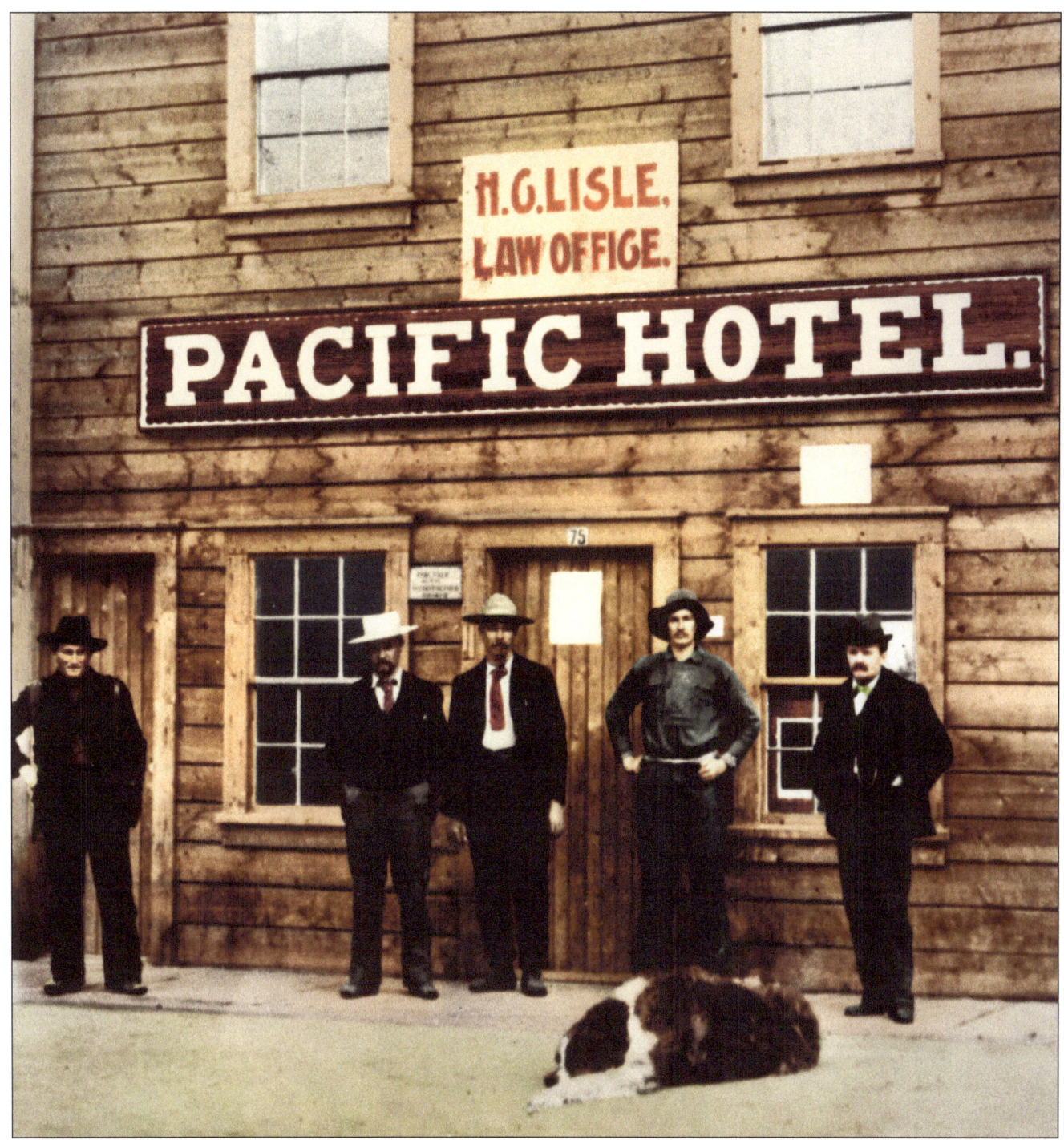

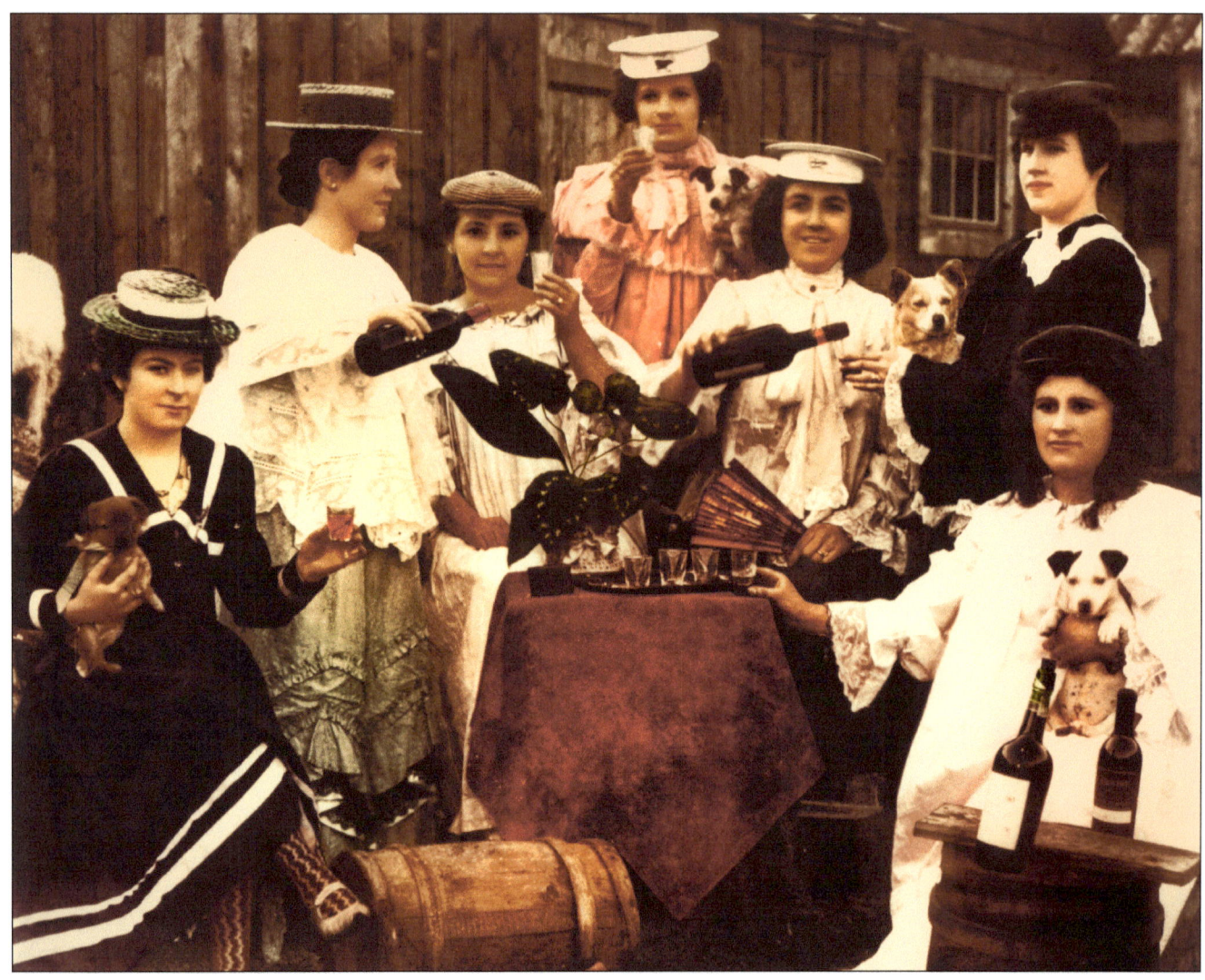

Above: Prostitutes, holding puppies, gathered for a "drinking bee" in the White Chapel district of Dawson. Like most mining towns, Dawson had a red light district.

Opposite: Cabins and caches are engulfed in the worst fire in Dawson's history on April 26, 1899. Unfortunately at the time the local fire brigade was on strike when a saloon caught fire. In total, 117 buildings were lost, including most of the Dawson's significant landmarks.

Fires were common in Dawson as the town was built and heated with wood and lit with candles and lanterns. Keeping water used for fire fighting from freezing was a significant challenge. It was a common strategy to drape adjacent buildings in wet blankets in an effort to prevent fires from spreading. This practice had limited success.

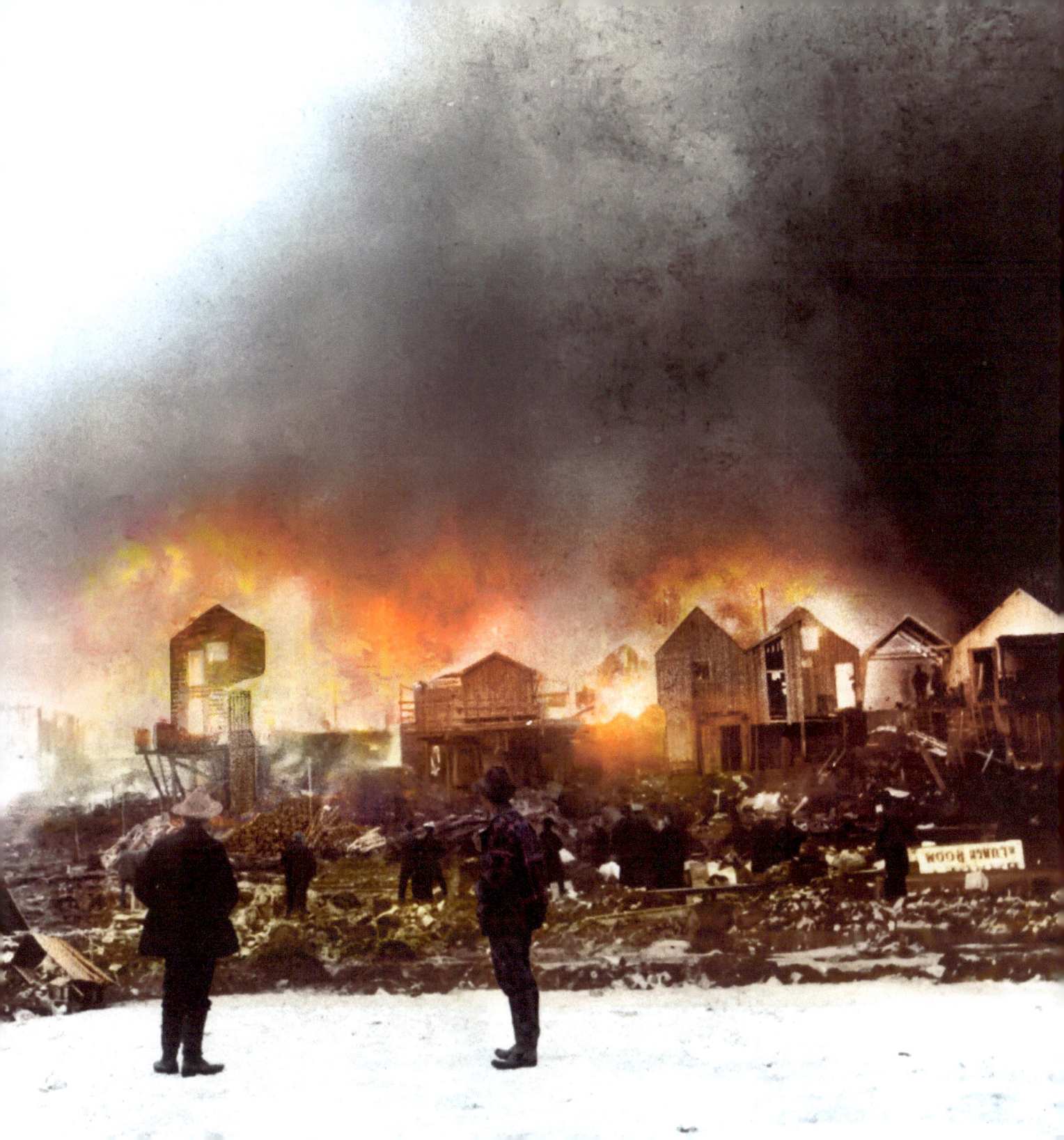

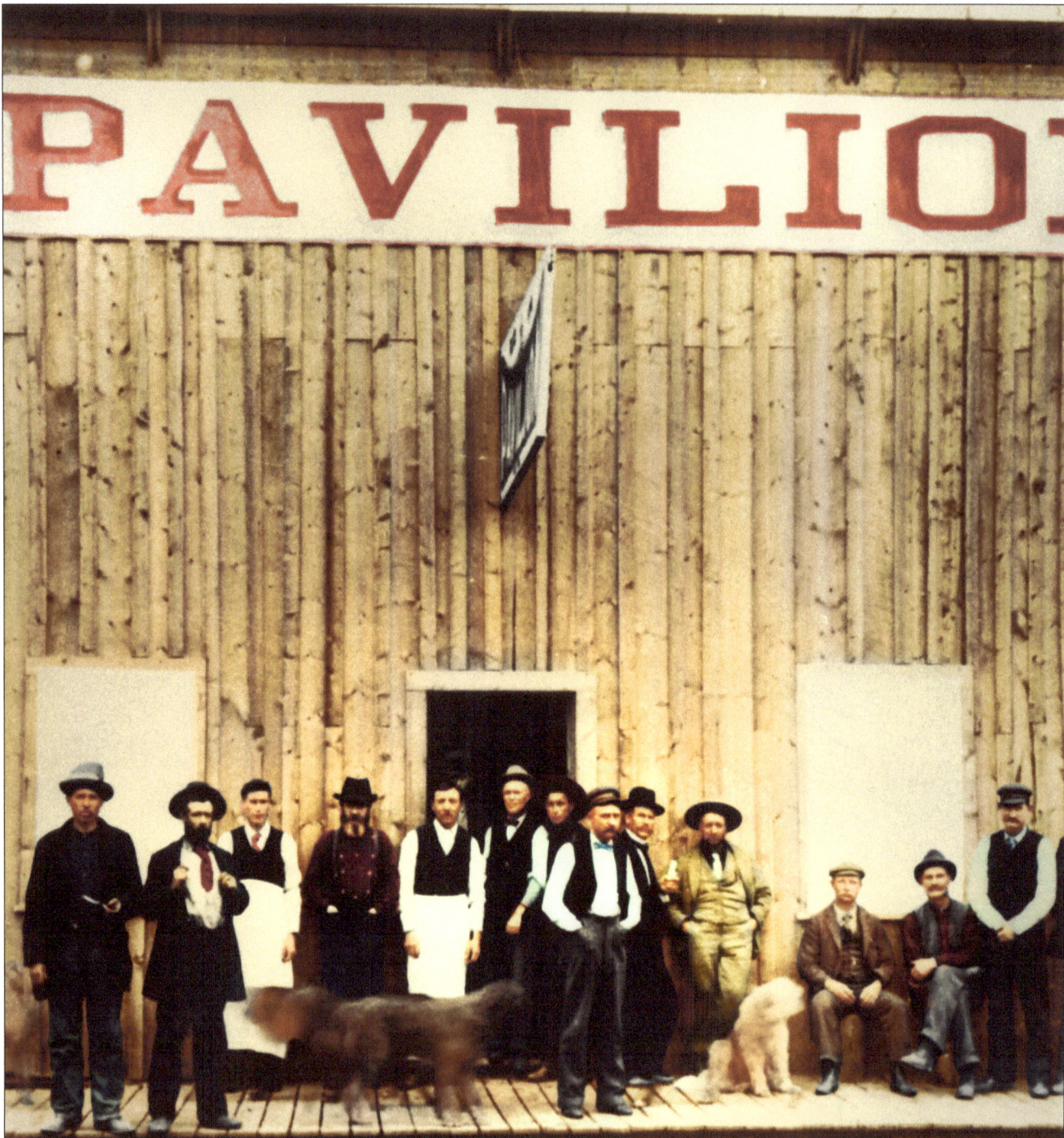

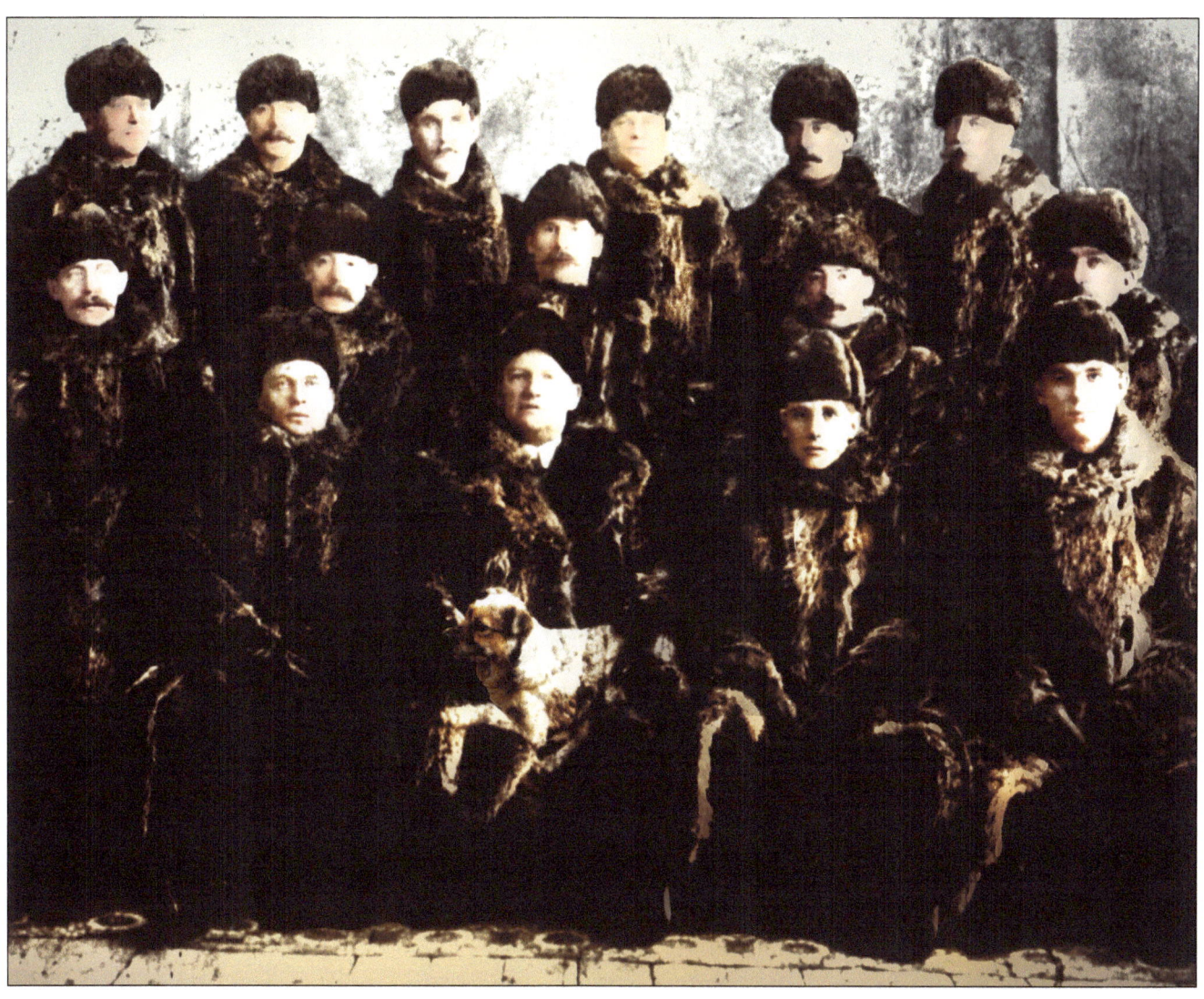

Above: Fifteen members of the North West Mounted Police in hats and full-length fur coats inside the town police station. By 1898 there was almost three hundred police in Dawson under the control of the legendary Sam Steele.

The North West Mounted Police maintained a close rein on the town. They freely sentenced people to the police barracks woodpile or, in the case of more serious offences, banished the convicted from the Klondike valley. Prostitutes could pursue their trade openly, and gambling halls held freedoms beyond anything seen on the continent. On the other hand, certain laws were enforced with great fervor. For instance, carrying guns was strictly forbidden and may have been the reason there was not a single murder in Dawson during the first summer of the rush.

Opposite: The elegant Pavilion Saloon on King Street.

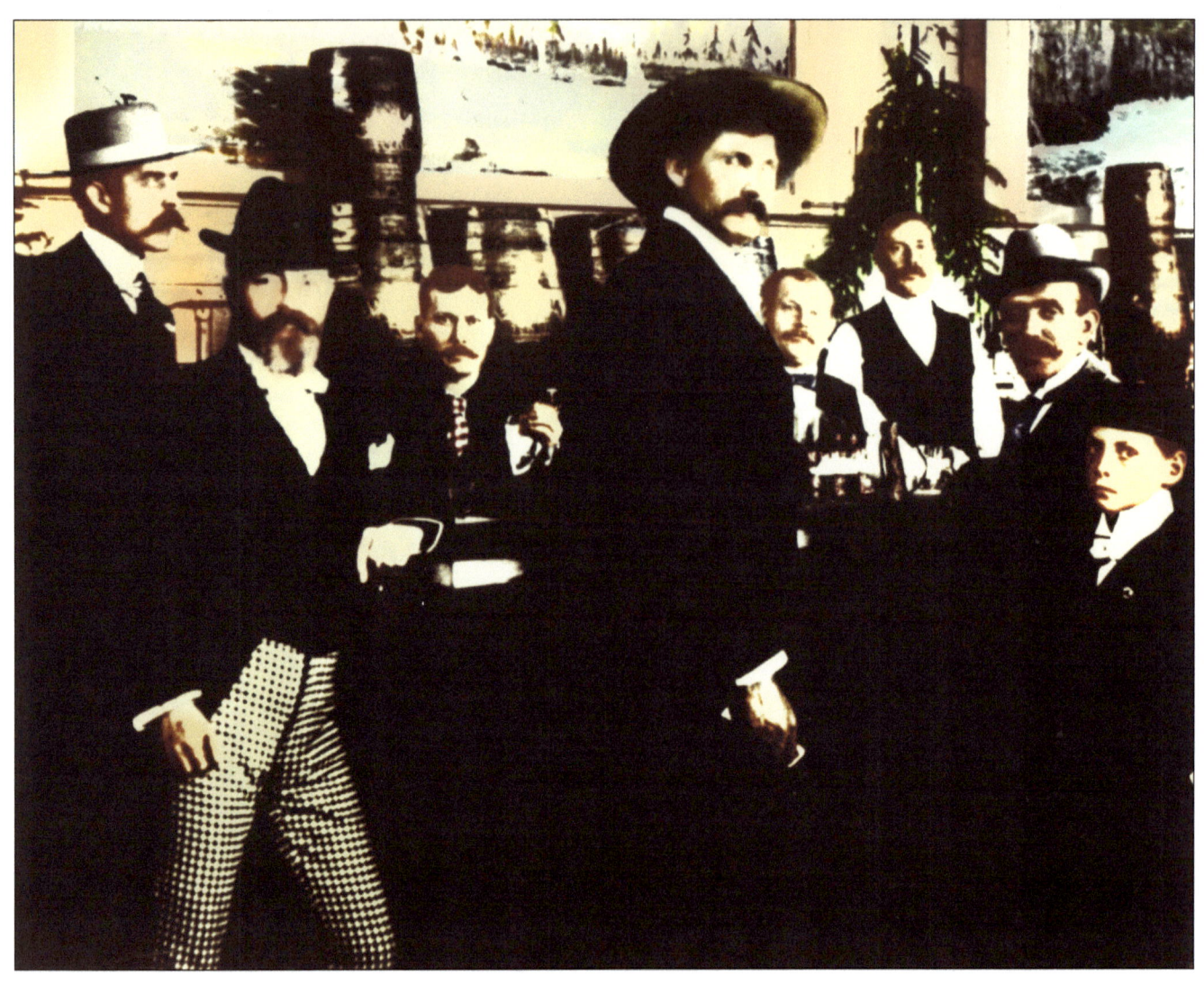

Above: Reopening of the Palace Grand Theater, which was destroyed by fire and reopened on July 7, 1899. The man with the wide-brimmed hat and wide-bowed moustache is "Arizona" Charlie Meadows. He was a legendary showman and sharp shooter and built the Palace Grand as an antidote to the rigors of the trail. Wood for the original building was salvaged from two paddlewheelers.

Opposite: The Palace Grand Theatre in celebration of St. Andrew's night in Dawson. It was customary for customers to howl like Malamutes when pleased with a performance.

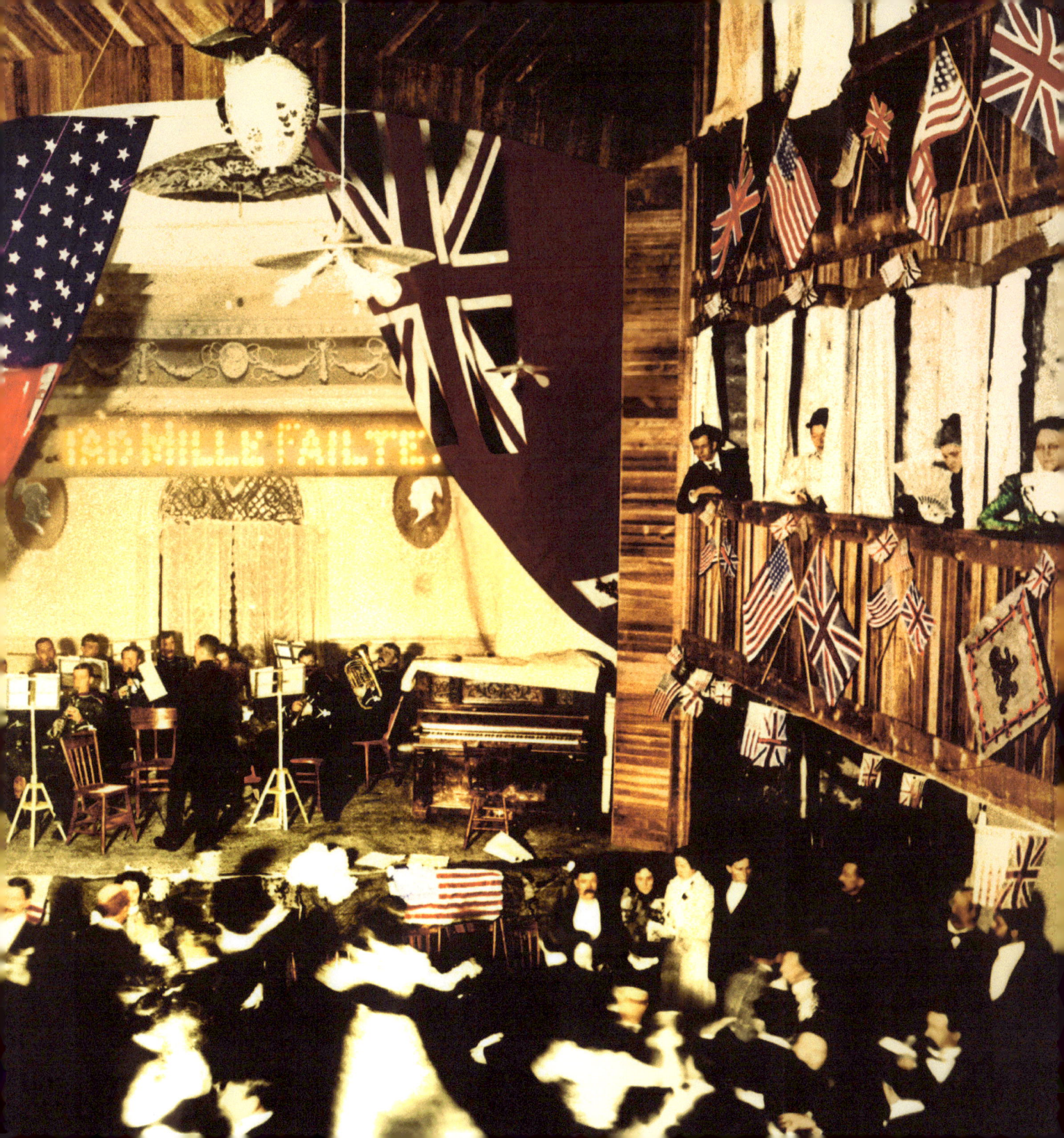

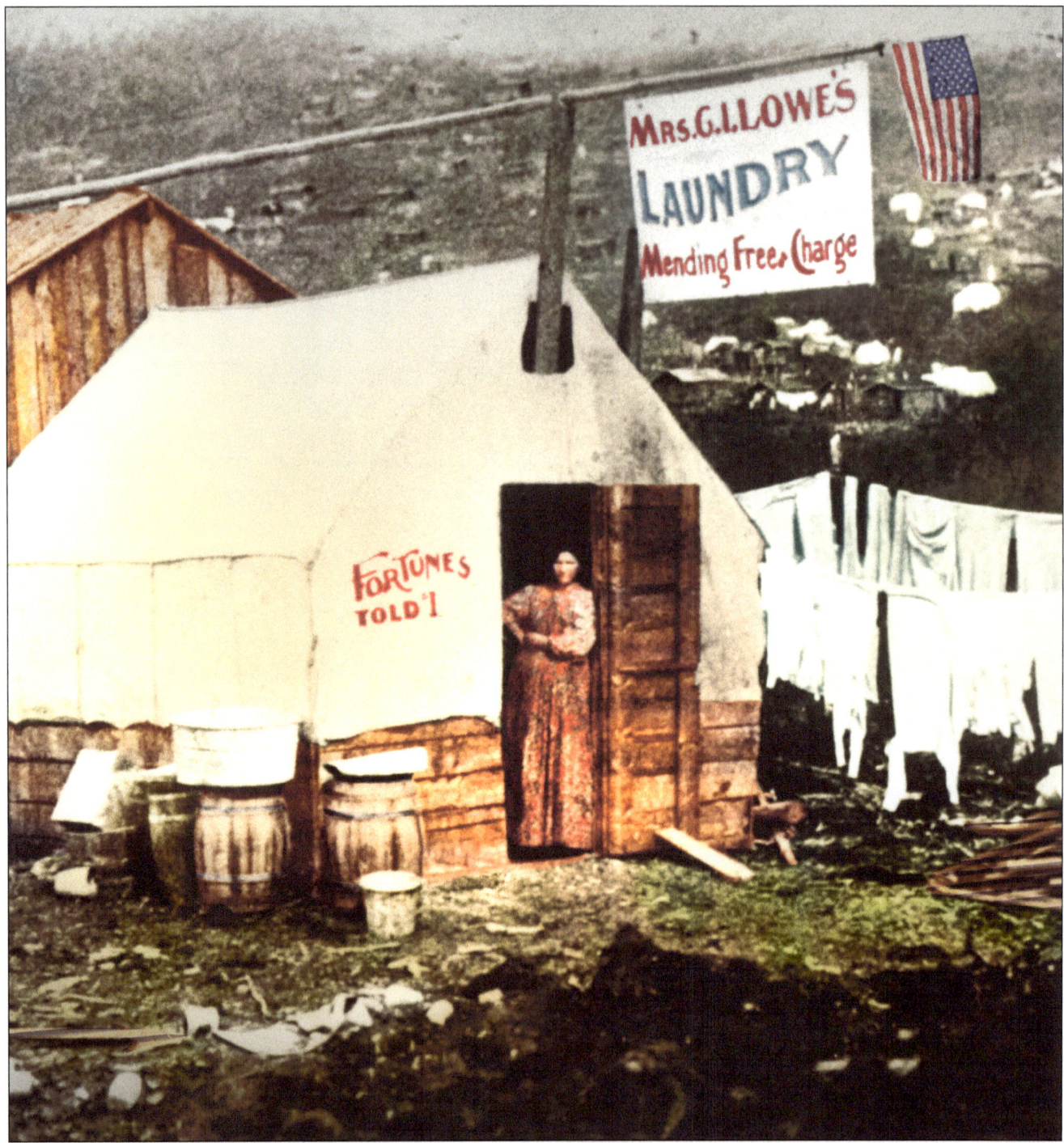

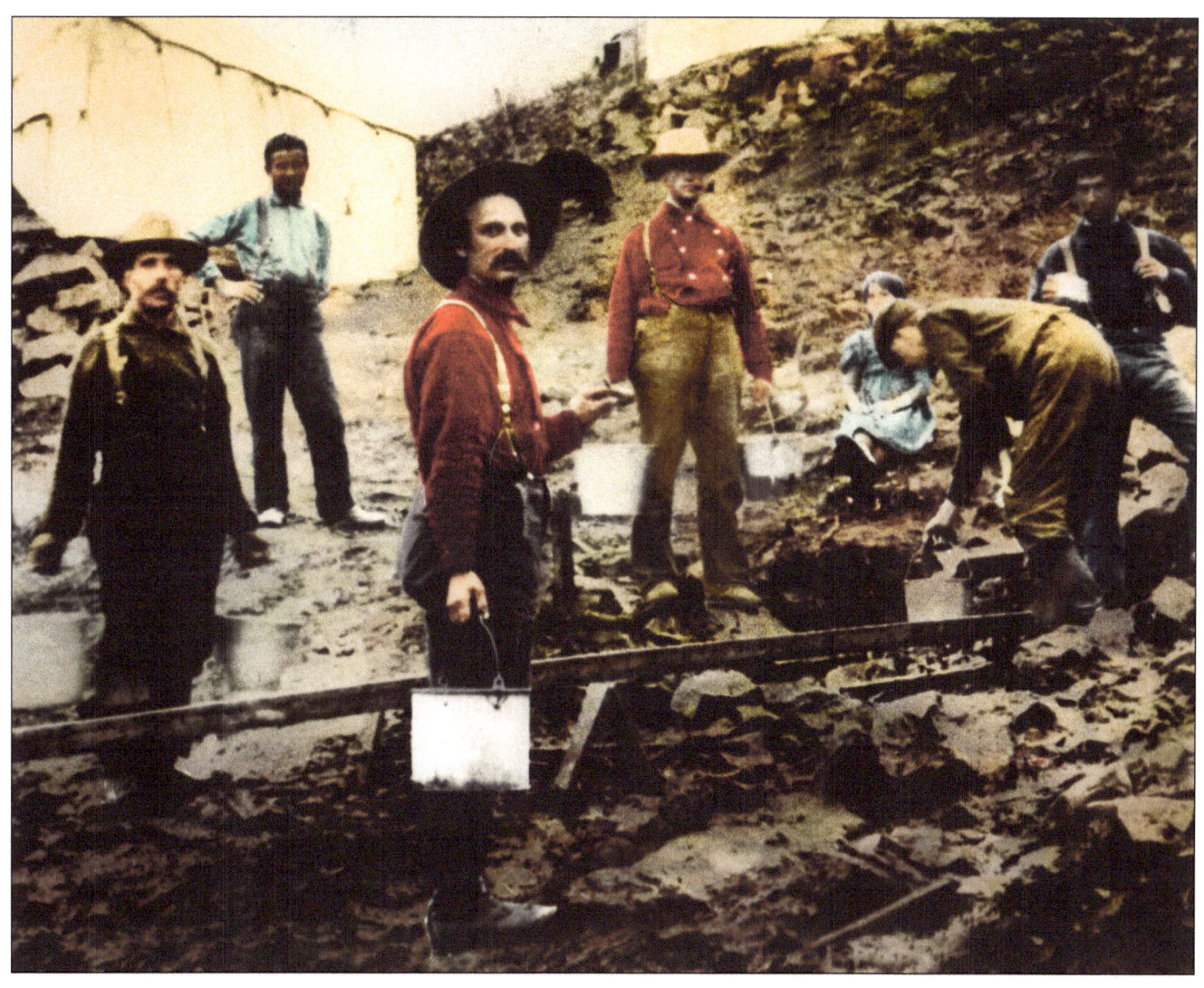

Above: In the Klondike, even simple chores like getting water were time consuming. The sediment-laden Yukon River was avoided for the creeks and streams of the region. However, even these water sources eventually became polluted and made many sick. Getting firewood required going even further afield.

Opposite: Mrs. G.I. Lowe's laundry on Bonanza Creek. She also did free mending and told fortunes. While less than ten percent of the Stampeders were women, many were successful entrepreneurs and provided valuable services.

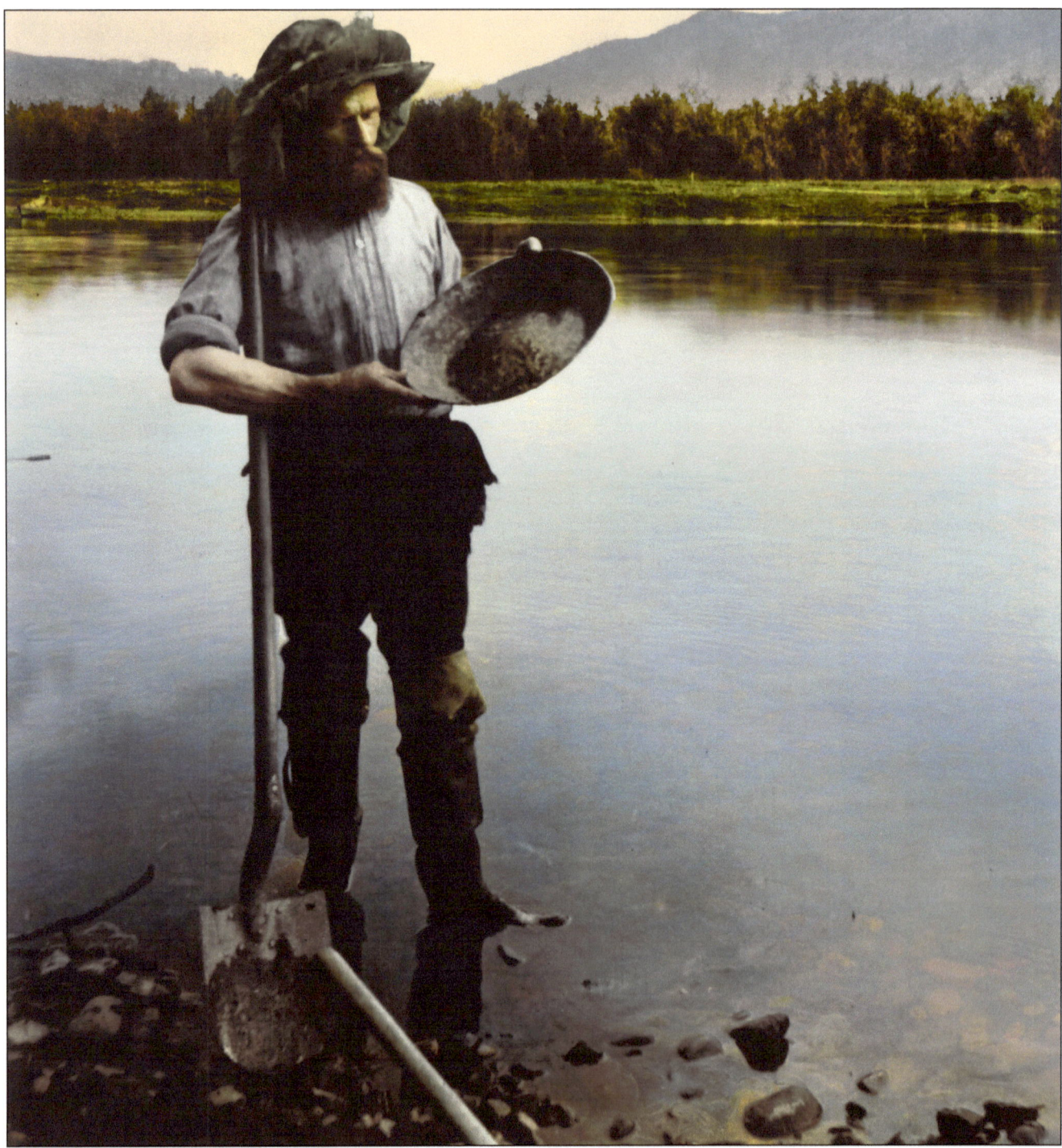

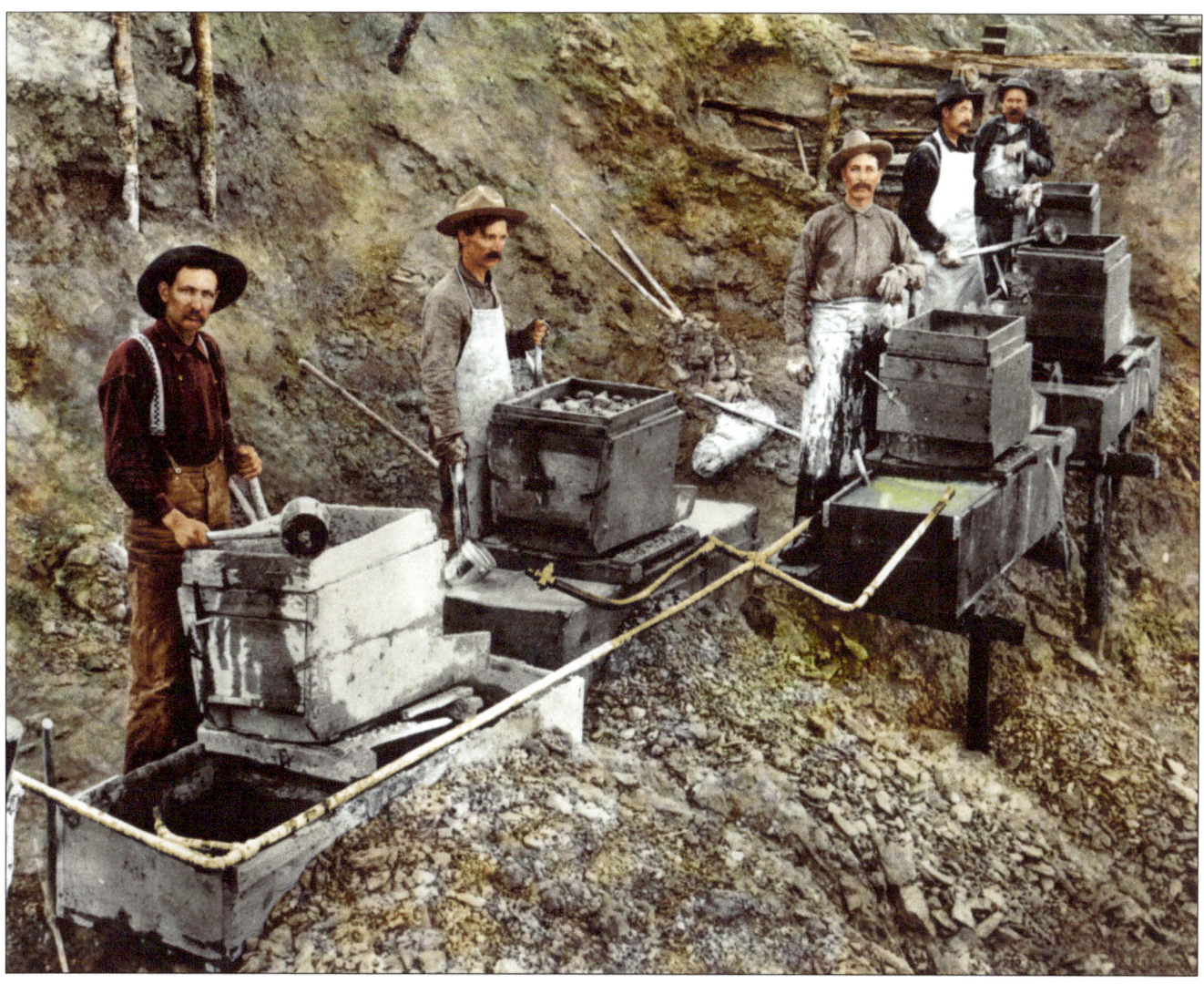

Above: Miners worked frantically with shovels and wheelbarrows. Rocker boxes had an insatiable appetite for gravel.

Opposite: The creeks of the Klondike region were described as being elaborately abundant. Stories outside the Yukon were of gold fields so rich you simply had to bend over and pick up nuggets. And while this was true for some of the richest claims at the start of the gold rush most people had to toil to get their gold.

The lone prospector swishing gold in a pan was the way the gold rush was described in the south. Initially, panning was the predominant means of extracting gold from the sands of the various creeks of the Klondike valley. With time, rocker boxes were constructed to sift the gravel more efficiently. The only limitation was one's ability to access enough gravel because most of the year the ground is frozen solid.

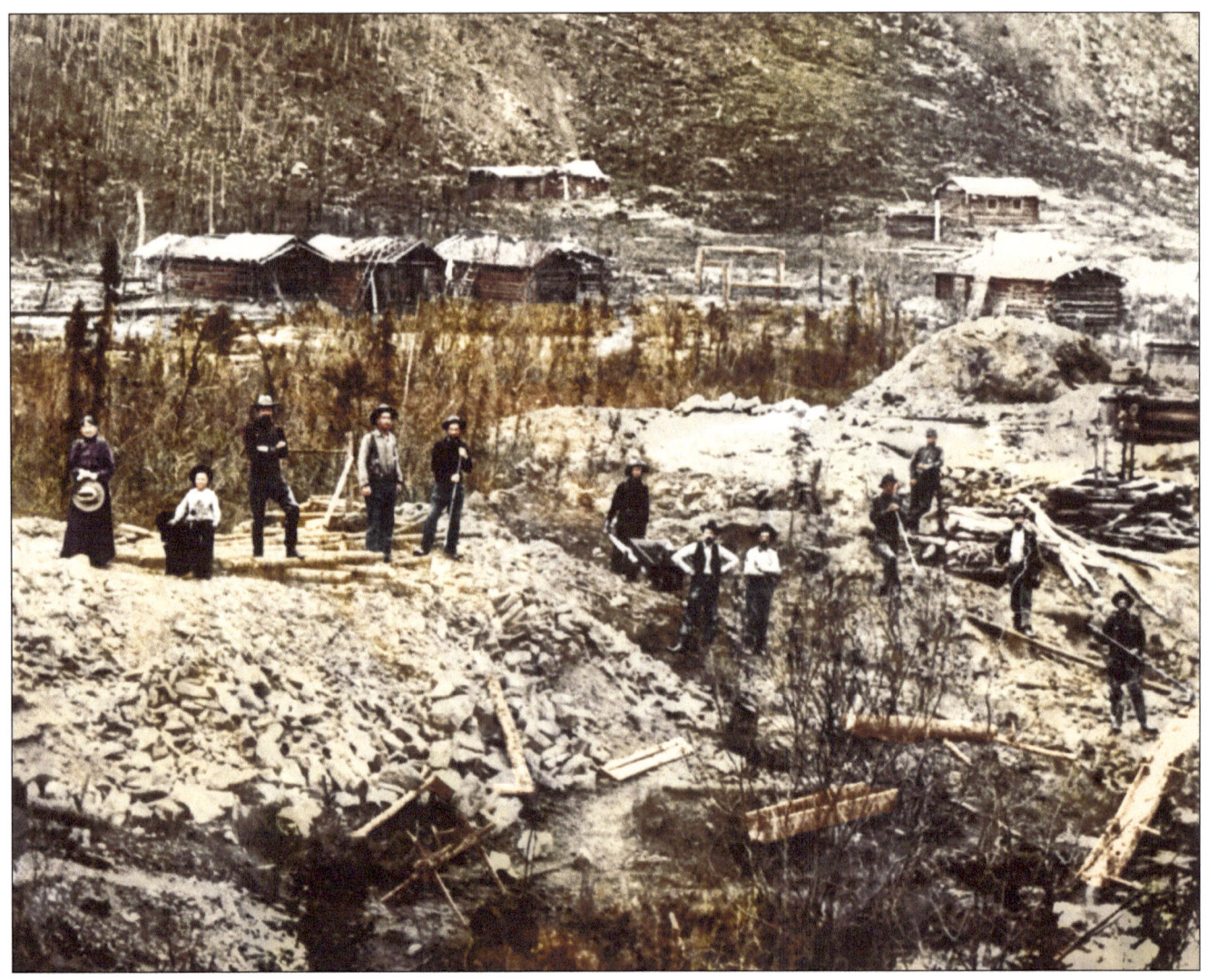

Above: Bonanza Creek was one of the richest creeks. Overnight the valley bottoms were transformed by the frenzy of mining activity.

Opposite: Water was essential for separating the gold from the gravel. Creeks were diverted or pumped into the mine sites.

Day laborers could make as much as $15 a day, and many received bonuses and other incentives to work as quickly as possible. Day laborers would never get rich, but they often did very well working these claims.

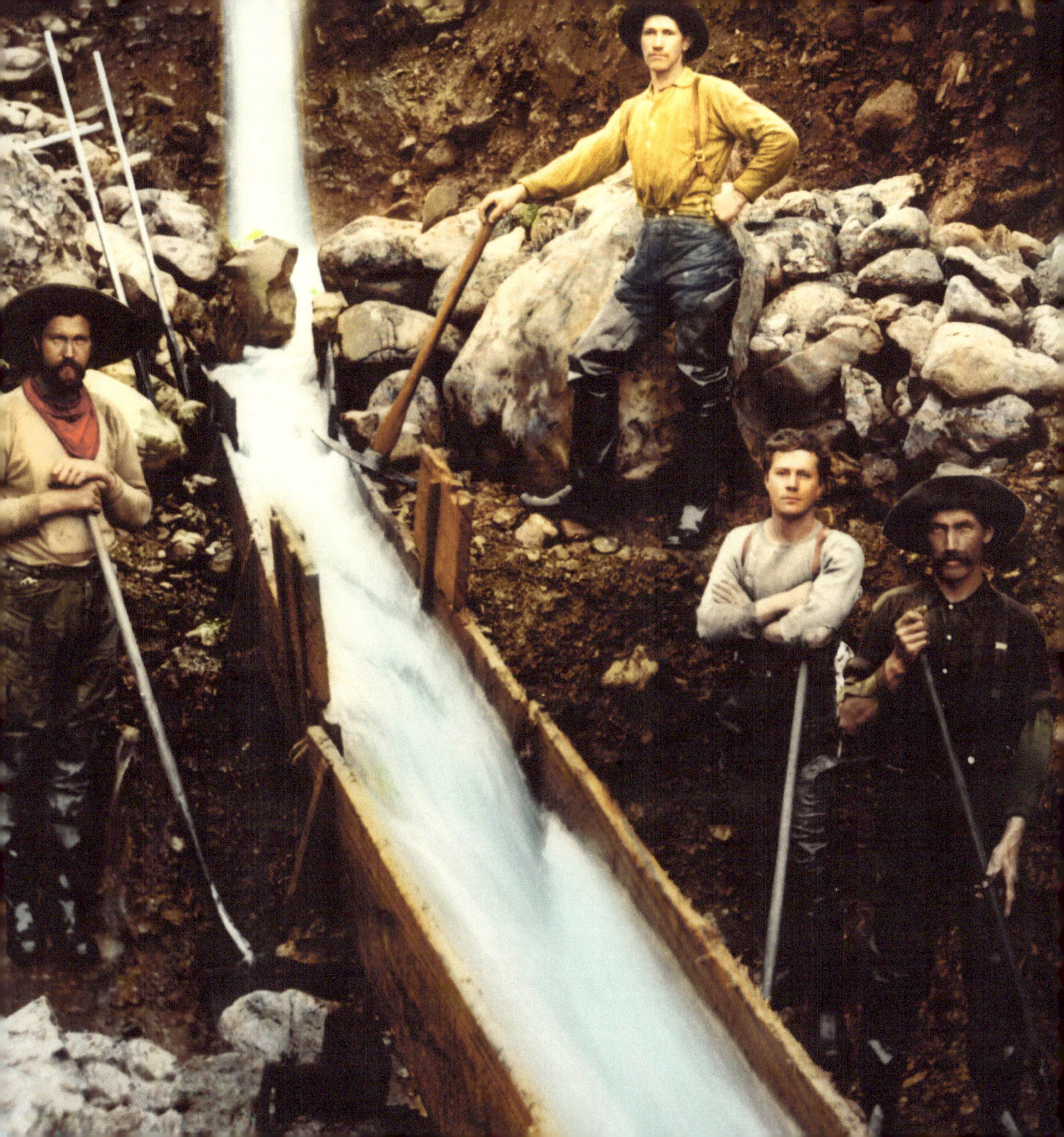

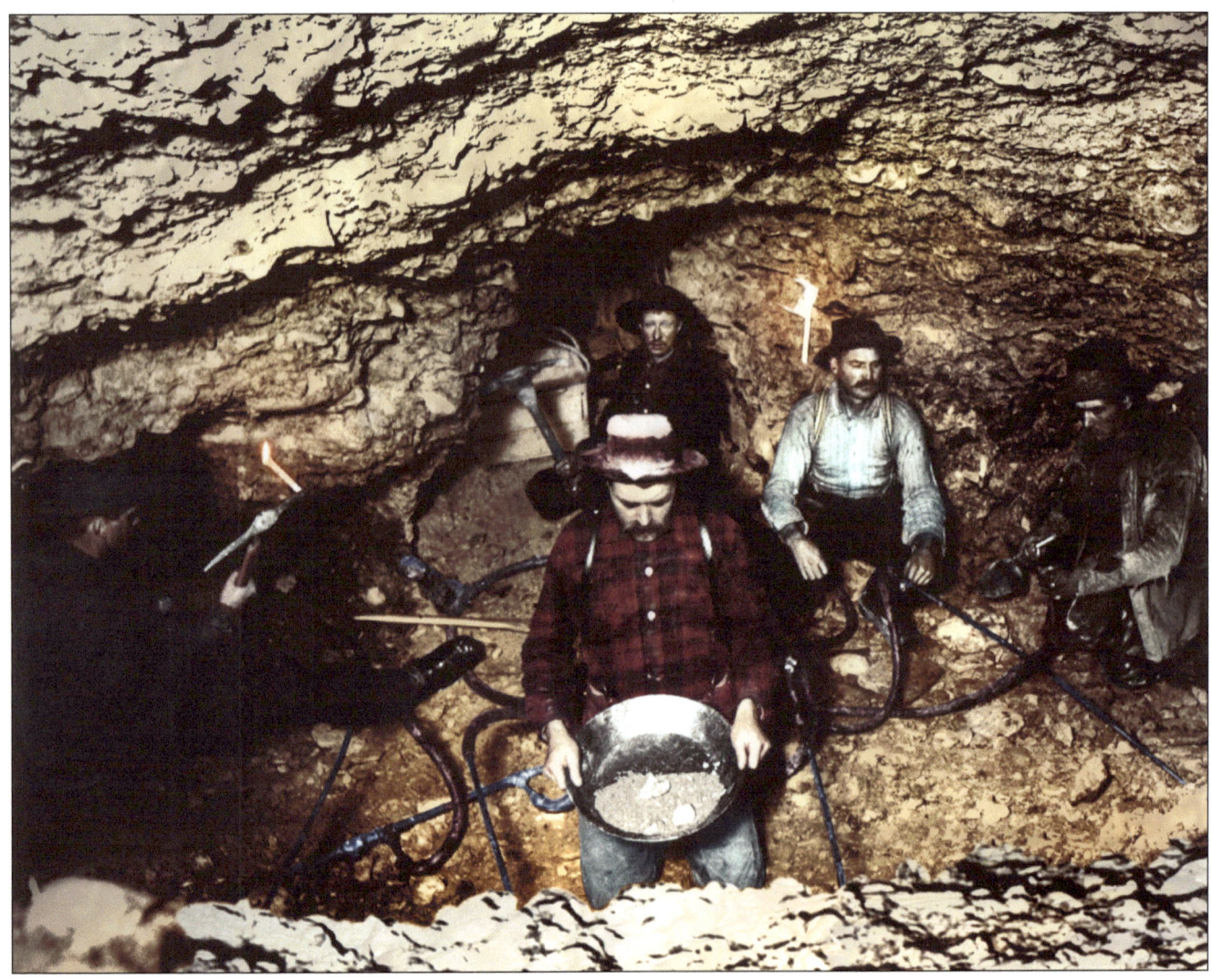

Above: Underground miners working with pickaxes; steam-thawing hoses are visible, as is the bucket to haul gravel to the surface. One miner is displaying a pan of pay dirt.

Opposite: Many searched for gold by going underground. Claustrophobic tunnels crisscrossed as Stampeders searched for a "pay streak." But the elusive "motherlode" was never found.

Tunnelling in the north is difficult because of the permafrost, a layer of earth that remains frozen throughout the year. Thawing this layer was done by setting large underground wood fires and then winching bucket after bucket of singed earth out of the mine. Once beyond the layer of permafrost, miners used pickaxe, shovel and bare hands to excavate. Candles flickered in the damp, narrow passageways. Most mines were more than thirty feet below the surface, and a few went deeper than a hundred feet.

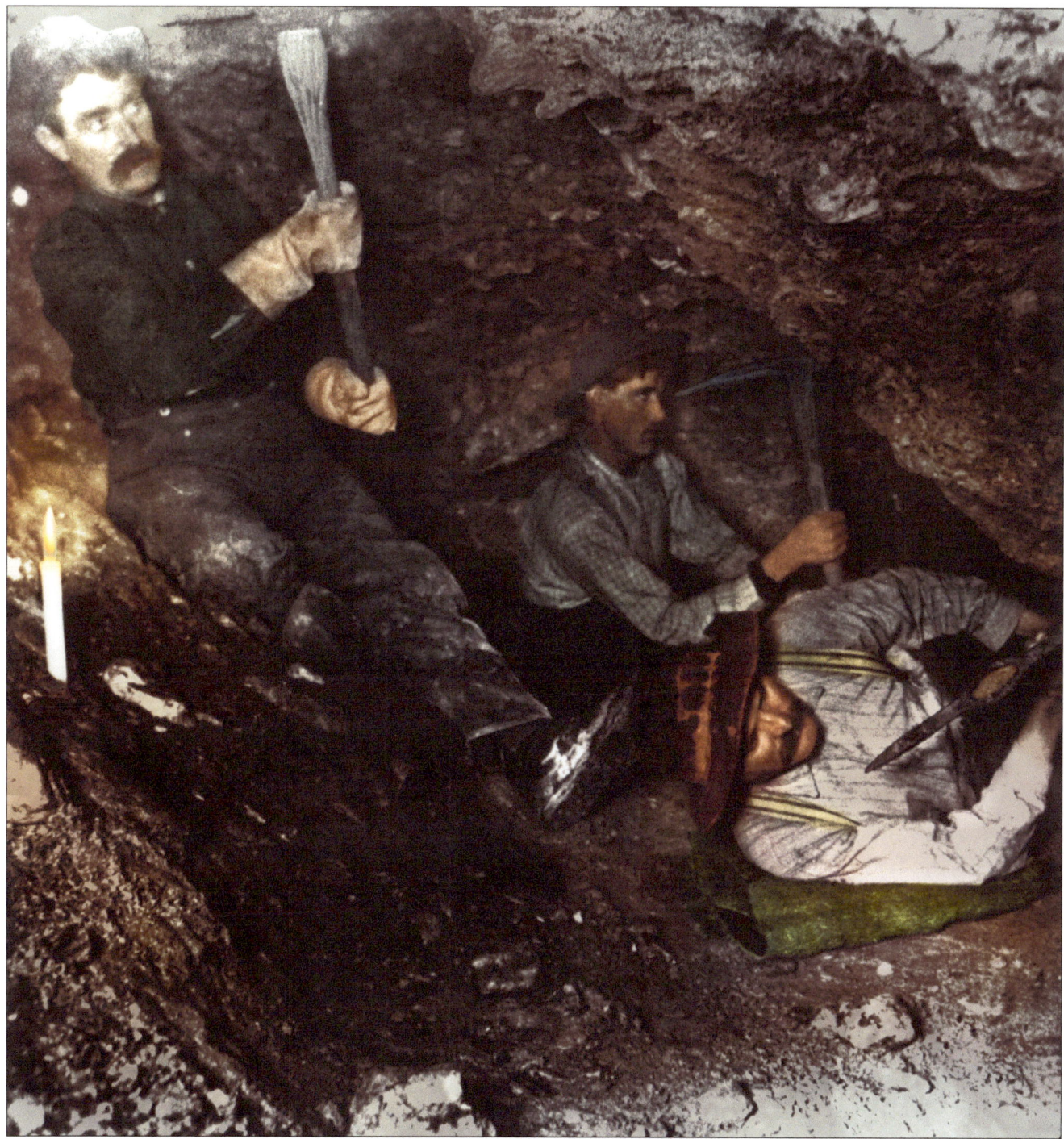

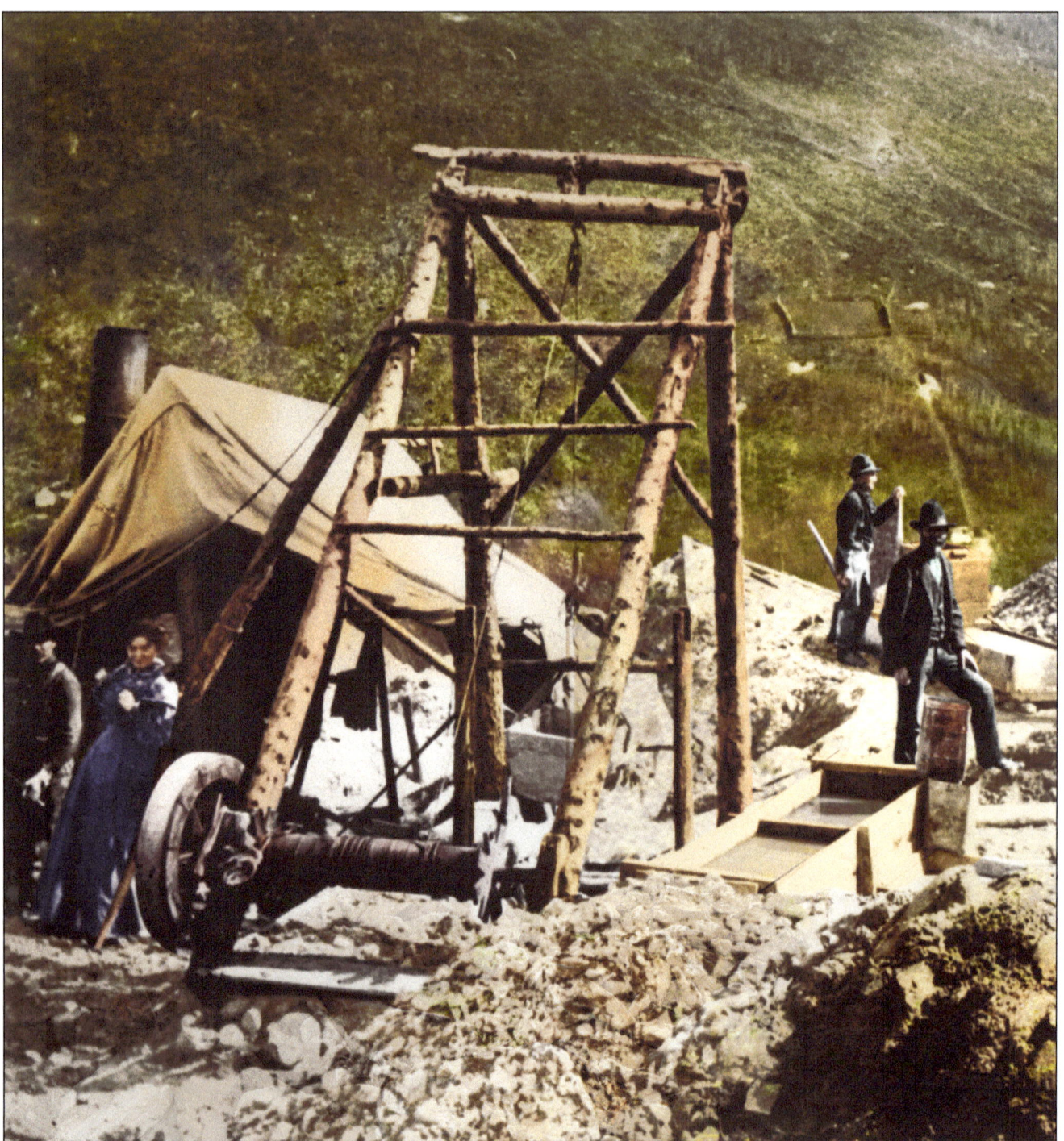

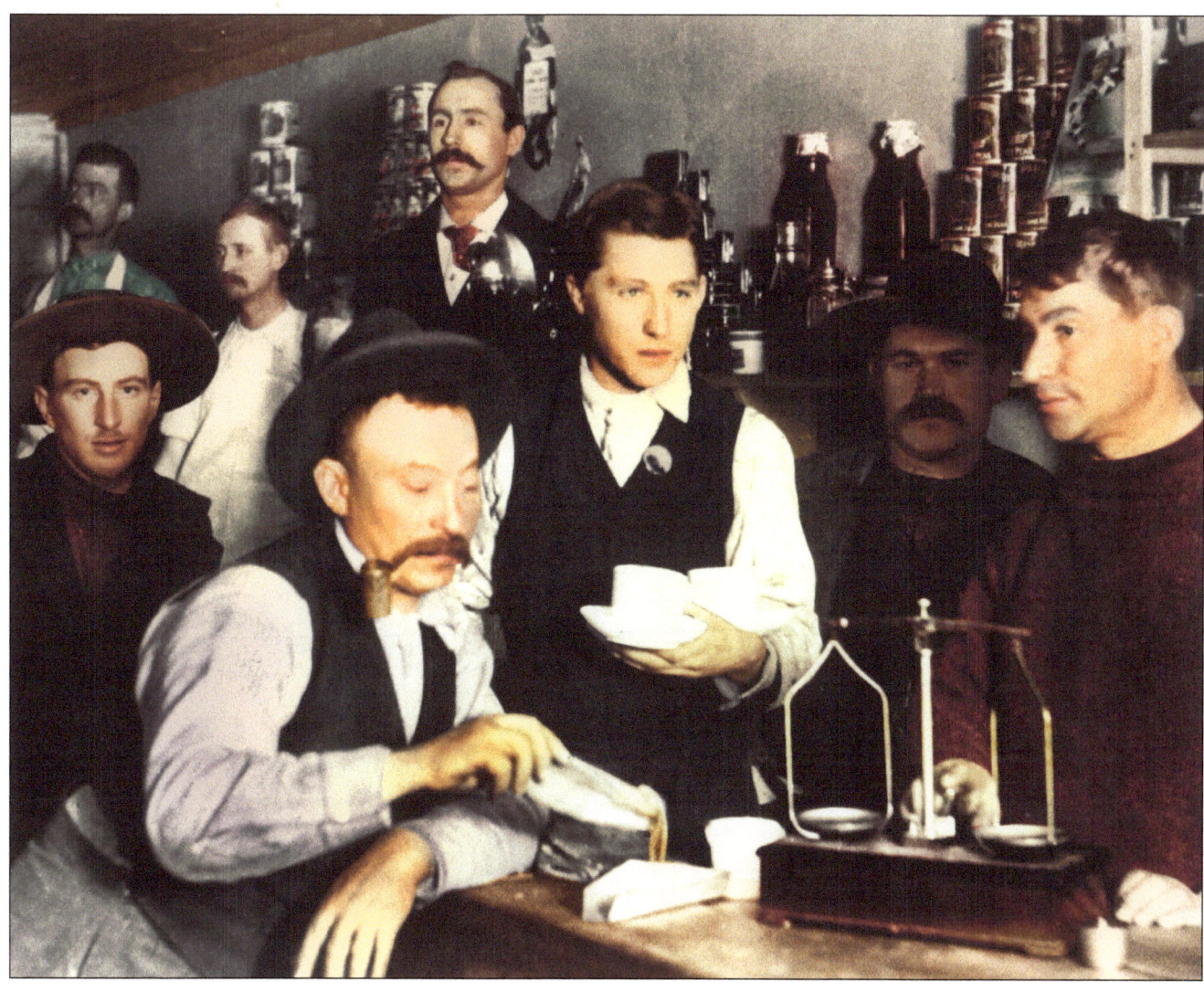

Above: Interior of a store with a man pouring gold dust from a pouch to be weighed on a set of gold scales on the counter. Pure gold dust was bought for $16 per ounce.

Opposite: Miners working a bench claim on Gold Hill. These sites were hastily built and hazardous for workers.

Page 64: Gold panner trying his luck. In August 1899, gold was discovered on the beaches of Nome, Alaska, and 8,000 people left Dawson in a week. Soon, Dawson was relatively deserted. Gold was still being mined, but large companies began buying claims from the small independent miners. The rocker boxes and sluices were replaced by enormous dredges. The dredges were less labor-intensive and those who worked them were employees, not owner-operators. The Klondike Gold Rush was over.

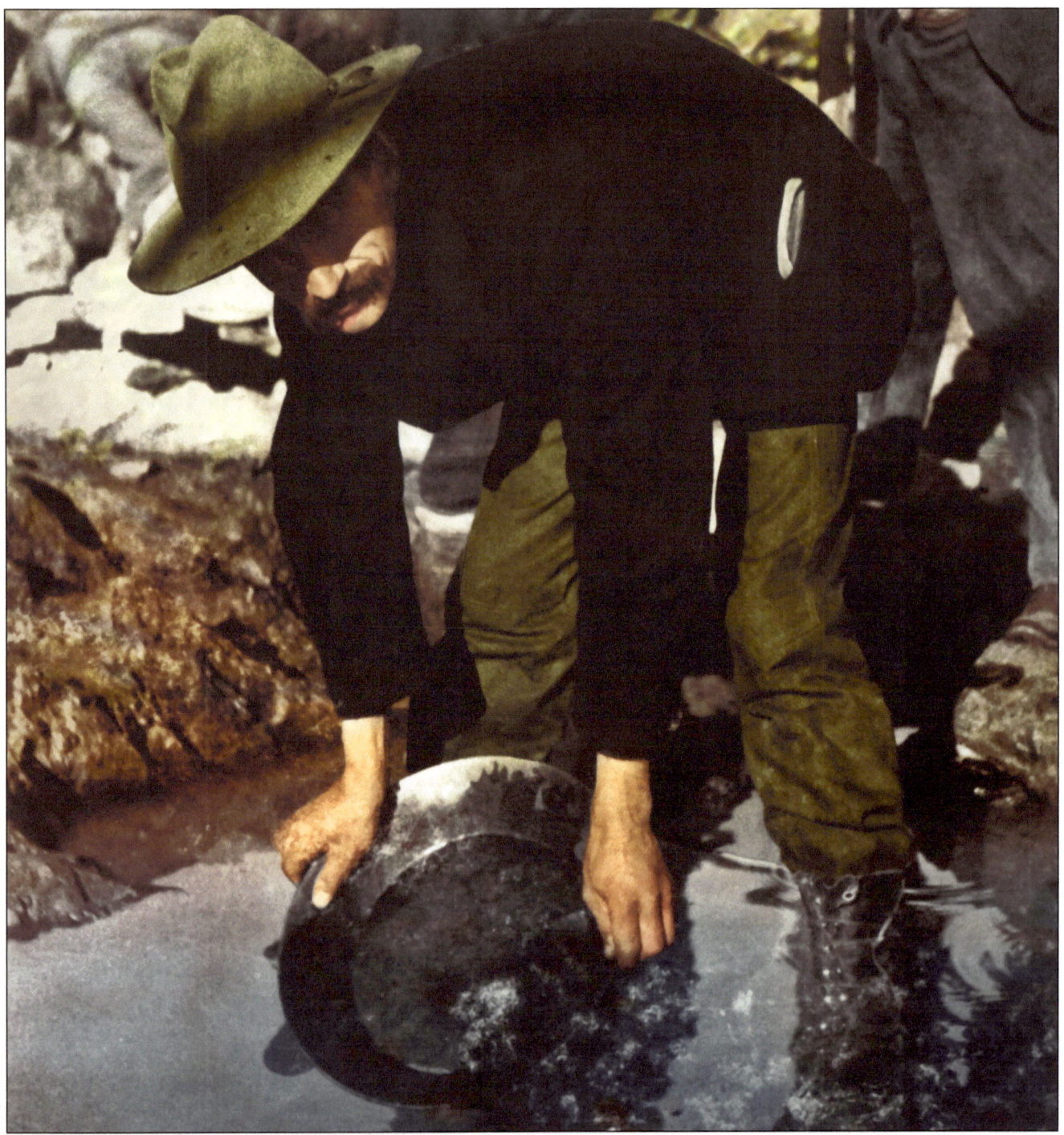